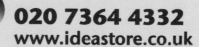

Library Learning Information

Idea Store® Canary Wharf
Churchill Place
Canary Wharf
London E14 5RB

020 7364 4332
www.ideastore.co.uk

**Created and managed by
Tower Hamlets Council**

need to know?

Children's Parties

Sean Callery

Collins

First published in 2006 by Collins
an imprint of
HarperCollins Publishers
77–85 Fulham Palace Road
London W6 8JB

www.collins.co.uk

Collins is a registered trademark of HarperCollins
Publishers Ltd

12 11 10 09 08 07 06
7 6 5 4 3 2 1

A catalogue record for this book is available from
the British Library

Produced by Lyra Publications
Managing editor: Emma Callery
Editor: Kate Parker
Designer: Bob Vickers
Photographer: Nikki English
Home economist: Sara Lewis
Stylist: Tessa Evelegh
Card designs: Laura Hines

For Collins
Series design: Mark Thomson

ISBN 0-00-721307-7

Colour reproduction by Colourscan, Singapore
Printed and bound by Printing Express Ltd, Hong Kong

Contents

Introduction

'We're having a birthday party' is a phrase that sends a shiver of anticipation and joy down the spine of a child, and possibly a shudder of horror through the whole body of the poor adult who's going to run it. But it doesn't have to be an ordeal.

Making the most of it

Holding a party can be stressful: the combination of organizing activities and food, and handling a group of excited children, keeping everyone happy and safe, is challenging. However, a good children's party (and that doesn't necessarily mean an expensive one) can be a wonderful event that strengthens friendships and leaves memories that last forever. Do remind yourself as you go through it: parties are supposed to be fun. After all, it's a fair bet that you remember some of your own birthday parties with a smile. Now it's payback time!

The most important voice is that of your child. After all, there's no point putting hours of work into something she don't really want. If you start by asking, 'What kind of party do you want?', you could be treated to some wild fantasy about taking the whole class for an elephant ride, and get the conversation off to a bad start. Instead, it's better to ask, 'What do you like at parties?' and find out what games and food she enjoyed. That will give you some idea of what you can suggest - it's always easier if you are able to give children choices to keep them involved in decisions.

Children are aware that birthdays are milestones in their lives, when they feel that bit more grown up, and, of course, when they get recognition and presents from those they love. Children also enjoy the colour and excitement of celebrations, the chance to do something different, and all the special attention in their honour.

The more involved children feel in planning a party, the more fun they will have.

What's it all about?

This book will help you because it offers advice on everything to do with children's parties, from where and when to have them to what games you could play, what food you might have, plus tips on the all-important cake. There are also 20 suggested party themes with ideas of how to use them at the party.

So, how can you ensure that your child and his guests have a great time, and you are still smiling as you close the door on the last child clutching their party bag?

Plan: Decide with your child what is going to happen and when, including a 'Plan B' for bad weather or other problems.

Prepare: Get organized in advance so that there is no last-minute panic a few hours before.

Keep your child involved: Give him meaningful jobs (like making the invitations) and discuss big decisions. That way you're much less likely to have complaints from him before, after (or worse, during!) the party.

Adapt: If it isn't working (and there is bound to be something), change it.

Now, where's that pack of balloons?

1 Planning your party

A good party for adults should be well planned, but a good children's party needs to be really very well planned and delivered, because when children don't understand what is happening and what is expected of them, you've got problems. This section takes you through the key questions of where and when your party should be, who to invite, and what to do at it. This will set you up for a party that your child, your guests and even you will be able to enjoy.

Where and when

You will need to decide early on where your party will take place. The obvious and by far the cheapest choice is: at home. However, for a variety of reasons, you may wish to consider other venues.

Where is best to hold a party?

Here are some reasons for not holding a birthday party at home:

▶ You don't want a large group of children running amok in your home. Any group of more than ten is likely to be too much for many houses, unless you have a large garden and are confident the weather will be good.

▶ You can't face the hassle of preparing and cleaning up afterwards. Parties mean hard work, and however many helpers you have, it will be happening in your home and that can feel like an invasion.

▶ You know you cannot handle the management of a group of children, and need someone to do the job for you. Managing children is not easy, and if it fills you with dread, it could spoil your life for weeks.

▶ You intend to invite lots of guests and so need a big space. Assess roughly how much space your child's friends are likely to need, and start searching for a party location.

▶ You've chosen a theme and the venue is perfect. For example, a water theme demands a pool location.

▶ You know of a good venue and trust it to as a place to hold a good party. Nothing beats personal experience or recommendation.

It is important that you consider the ages of the children involved. Most are likely to be the same age as your child, so if you blanch at the idea of ten 'clones' of her rushing into your kitchen, consider other locations. However, the venue should be appropriate to the age and nature of the children involved: some find swimming pools big and frightening, for example. Similarly, a softball park can be a noisy and scary environment for young or nervous children. Remember, too, that a party venue that can take your booking is quite likely to have other parties going on either at the same time (which can be confusing for guests and staff) or just before or after, so you could feel hurried or have to wait while the staff clear up.

Another consideration is where the venue is and how you expect people to get there and back. Will parents have to deliver children there, and collect? This is not practical or polite if the journey is long. Maybe you could organize help with transport from friends, or use public transport (you'll need lots of helpers) or even hire a minibus.

Check rooms before you hire them, and be very clear about whether there will be staff that are only there to deal with your group while you're there.

Wet games must be played outside, which is also best for lively group games.

Home options

If you find a good venue in terms of activities, but are not sure about the quality or quantity of the food they offer (some seem to slice the cake into minute portions), you could start the party at one place, then come back home to eat or play. That would take some of the pressure of being the host away from you, but still leave you feeling that you've made a big contribution to the success of the party. It would also save money.

Another option is to have the party at your house, but with it all happening outside, provided there is space to play and eat. So if your garden can take it, or you have a pool or hot tub, you could still be the host without having to get the vacuum cleaner out at all!

Venue ideas

Here are some suggestions of the types of venue that could host your party:

Bowling alley: A popular location where it is fairly easy to keep a group together, but not cheap.

Community centre or village hall: Often has a room you can book for a reasonable fee, then you can decorate it yourself (don't forget you'll need to take it all down again!) and serve your own food.

Craft shop: Some shops host parties where children make cards or other crafts. For the right children, this is a novel and stimulating choice.

Farm: Some farms welcome visitors and are perfect if you have an animal theme for your party. Some also offer horse and cart rides to a picnic site where children can also let off steam.

Ice rink: Some children will love this, but you could be on tenterhooks about where they are and whether everyone is safe.

Leisure or sports centre: Great for sporty parties, and staff should be able to organize games for you.

Local park: Convenient to get to, but you won't have it to yourself, and will need to set clear rules about where children can and should not go.

Museum: Many museums are very well geared to entertaining children, and some will let you book a sleepover party. Not always cheap, and your more lively guests may find the environment restricting.

Paintball venue: Exciting and novel for older children, but pricey and bound to stimulate competitiveness, which can be rather ugly.

Restaurant: Fast-food venues are very well set up to run a party for you, but you might feel as if you are on a kind of party conveyor belt, with nothing being individual to your child. If your wallet can stand it, taking a group of children to a pizza restaurant can make a lovely, low-stress party.

Soft-play centre: Great for lively play, but there will be lots of other children there so you may spend all your time perched anxiously by the barrier, making sure your group is OK.

Zoo: Great for kids; very bad for your bank balance.

When to hold the party

When will you have the party? That might seem a silly question (on the birthday, of course!), but it may be better all round to have the party on a different day. Weekends are generally better than weekdays as both children and parents have fewer commitments, such as after-school activities, so they are more likely to be free.

Time of day

▶ Assuming the party is being held at your home, you need to allow two to three hours for it (the lower figure suits younger children: they'll get tired and fractious after a couple of hours).

Time	Advantages
8–10am	Have a breakfast party! Children can come (in their nightclothes if they like) for breakfast, with cake of course.
12–3pm	You will have the rest of the day to tidy up and recover.
4–7pm	Gives you plenty of preparation time, but organize your evening meal in advance so you don't have to cook, exhausted, next to a pile of cake crumbs.
7–10pm	Good for older children, but that doesn't leave a lot of clearing-up time before you clamber into bed with a sigh of relief.

Whatever time you consider, think through how each guest will get to and leave the party, and whether you'll need to walk or drive children home or ask their parents to collect them.

▶ If the birthday falls in a holiday, some guests could be away and would have to miss it. It can also be harder to contact families if they are away.

▶ If you are booking an entertainer or equipment like a bouncy castle, they tend to be booked up more at weekends than weekdays.

Having the birthday party on a different day to the actual birthday allows you to have a quiet(ish) family celebration at the time, knowing there will also be an all-singing, all-dancing party with friends. What child can complain about celebrating his birthday twice? Since many of the friends are likely to be from school, it is easier to set up a party during term-time when you are likely to see parents to make arrangements.

A breakfast party can follow a sleepover or be a party in its own right – it needn't start at 8am!

Who to invite?

Choosing the guests can be agonizing for children. They know how highly their peers value party invitations, and will not want to hurt children by not inviting them (and don't even consider trying to keep the party a secret – it won't, and you could offend lots of people).

How many do you want to invite?

Start by considering how many children the venue can safely hold. Commercial venues will probably take any number for a price, so if you really want to invite the whole class from school, go for one of these. If the party is at your home, any number up to about 12 should be about right, but if you are near that limit, make sure that you have at least one other adult to help out. School groups work on a ratio of one adult to six children, and that is a good rough guide. Without doubt, the larger the group, the more work it is, and not necessarily the more fun it is for anybody.

Some parents stick to a rule of 'one child for every year of age' so that a four-year-old has four guests, and so on, but that may not be practical. Others opt to keep everyone happy by inviting the whole class, but that may not be feasible or desirable! A whole class might rub along and cooperate well under the watchful eye of their teacher, but may not be as amenable outside school. Young children in particular can be upset at seeing a horde of children descend on their favourite toys. Many children have a recognizable 'friendship group' who play together, but you can't guarantee that your child really likes everyone in that group (girls especially tend to have strong preferences).

Narrowing it down

Agree a rough number of guests with your child, then decide on the 'must invites': best friends and close relatives. As you build your list from here, consider the following points:

▶ Who else will he know at the party? Knowing no one else could be pretty miserable for some children.

▶ Did your child go to his party? It seems only polite to invite him back, unless, of course, you've got a good reason not to.

▶ Does he like parties? Some children don't particularly enjoy being in groups and you would be better off inviting them for a separate sleepover or other activity.

▶ Do you want a mix of boys and girls? Some children tend to mix with others of the same gender, but others have friends of both sexes. However, being the only girl or boy at a party is a 'no no' for most children, so you'll want to invite at least a pair of the opposite sex, if at all.

▶ Apart from school, think about other groups your child may be part of, like Brownies or Beavers, gym or swimming clubs and so on. There may well be children she likes in these groups too.

Guests should know at least one other child who has been invited, or they may feel left out.

good to know

Joint parties
One idea that can make life easier is to pair up with another family. Find out if your child's birthday is near that of any of his friends and consider linking up. This is especially good if they have mutual friends. You can then share the work of planning, preparing and running the party. It is important that both children are happy with the arrangement, as an upset party host is never a pretty sight or experience.

What will happen at the party?

Now you arrive at the important question of 'What will we actually do at the party?' Don't assume that the children will be happy occupying themselves at a party: they won't, at least not for long. With a group of excited children who do not necessarily know each other well, you will have to keep them occupied.

Keep it right for the age

Children up to the age of five will most likely just enjoy the party as an occasion. As long as you've got the basic ingredients of a few simple games, food and a cake, they'll be happy. They have fairly short attention spans so they need lots of short activities and they probably aren't that bothered about a theme.

Between the ages of six and nine, children are familiar with the party basics and will relish the novelty of variations in activities and, especially, themes. They've got lots of energy so you need to give them a chance to let off steam and run about, and they'll enjoy lively games.

Children aged 10–14 still enjoy parties but these children really need the stimulation of a theme, especially if it gives them a chance to dress up. They can play more complicated games (which still need to be supervised), but given the excuse, they often love the chance to play at being young again (plenty of 14-year-old girls will still relish a teddy bear party, half as a joke, half in the same way they did ten years ago).

Hiring entertainers

Bring in an entertainer and all you have to worry about is the food and perhaps a few games. It costs, but for some parents it is worth every penny. If you are worried about managing a group of children, this could be your answer. Just be sure the entertainer is right for your age group. Some possibilities are:

must know

Important decisions
Key questions are:
▶ Are you going to have a theme? See pages 24–65.
▶ What are you going to do about food? See pages 144–71.
▶ How are you going to entertain the children? Read on!
▶ If it's games, see page 94–141.

Clown: A clown is good entertainment value for six- to nine-year-olds. Younger children can find clowns frightening, and older kids may find them very tame.

Magician: Can provide brilliant entertainment; excellent for larger groups.

Puppet show: Very popular with younger children.

Hiring equipment

Bringing in something special for the party makes it more of an event, but you'll still have to run the show. Possibilities include:

Book an enertainer, and you've got a party highlight to work around.

Bouncy castle: Great fun for kids but needs to be supervised.

Bubble machine: A good way of adding novelty, but it does wear off.

Disco: For the right children, noisy bliss.

DVD or video: Choose the right film and you've got happy, involved, quiet children. However, you can almost guarantee that at least one child will have seen it several times before.

Karaoke: Kids who like to perform will love it. Don't expect everyone to be keen to step up and sing, however.

Parachute: Great for games. You might be able to borrow one from a local children's group.

Soft-play equipment such as play tunnels: Young children will love it, but you'll need to have space for it all.

Trampoline: Like the bouncy castle, fun but needs supervision. You may be able to borrow one.

Sleepovers

Sleepovers are part of modern childhood. Children of both sexes and of sometimes surprisingly low ages stay over at their friends' houses at weekends and sometimes after parties. The host child gets all the fun of having their friends to play with for hours, often well into the evening and night. The host family have to tolerate this invasion with grace and dignity.

Plan carefully

Since birthday parties can be emotionally and physically exhausting, a sleepover that same night may seem a poor idea. It also sets up the problem of whether some guests are invited to the party, but not to the subsequent sleepover. This is likely to cause division and upset. However, if your child is particularly keen on sleepovers, you could suggest that the birthday party comes in the form of one.

Sleep is low down on the list of priorities for a sleepover!

► Keep the numbers lower than for a standard party: certainly less than ten and preferably between four and six.

► There is more scope for 'fallings out' during sleepovers than during a birthday party – children tend to be left alone to chat, some of them feeling emotionally vulnerable because of the strange location.

► A major attraction of the sleepover is the chance to stay up late. Do not expect children to go to sleep at anywhere near their usual time, and do not expect them to obey your requests to go to sleep! Ideally, put them in a room a long way from your own bedroom: then you won't hear the chat and excited squawks.

Sleeping arrangements

Ask children to bring their own bedding or sleeping bag, so that they have their familiar things and you don't have to put extra loads through the washing machine. A comforter and torch would also help in addition to nightclothes and a toothbrush.

Sleepovers are all about change in routine, so you could put everybody into a different room than usual (a living room festooned with chair cushions is ideal). If you do use a bedroom, you could suggest that everybody sleeps somewhere 'different', such as under the bed, or in one huge nest.

The midnight feast

A 'midnight feast' is an important part of the sleepover ritual for some. It needn't be at midnight and it certainly shouldn't be a feast! Choose foods that won't mark or leave too many crumbs in bedding, so raisins rather than chocolate, and cut-up fruit rather than crisps. Of course you will want to add a few treats like sweets, but don't supply too many as washing the bedding of a child who has been sick is no fun whatsoever.

Avoid giving fizzy drinks or other drinks with caffeine in them because that will keep the children up even longer. Serve drinks in lidded containers to avoid spillages. You could deliver

Makeover fun

Two ideas for sleepovers with a difference are:

▶ A makeover party where everybody brings some make-up and takes it in turns to give someone a makeover. You could add to the fun by asking the children to do their own make-up – but without mirrors.

▶ A bedding makeover party, where children bring a plain pillowcase and you supply them with fabric pens with which to decorate them. You'll need to agree this with the other parents in advance!

the 'feast' with some ceremony at a time that suits you, or even leave it in a cool box for the children to open up. Keep a light on in the hallway so that children can find their way to the bathroom.

Lights out!

When you retire to bed, it is a fair bet that the sleepover children will still be telling scary stories or sharing secrets, so stick to a polite request to keep the noise down rather than insist they all go to sleep: they won't.

If possible, provide a 'bolt hole' of a different room where it is agreed anyone who wants privacy or has had enough of the noise can bed down, but this should be respected as a silent place.

I want to go home

Sometimes the idea of a sleepover is more fun than the reality. Children away from familiar surroundings can get homesick, especially when deprived of their usual routines. Talk to parents of children to be invited to check if they are confident their child is ready for the experience. If the child has not spent a night away from home before – say, with grandparents or on a school residential trip – he may find the reality daunting and you will be faced with a weepy young guest. You could always suggest that such children could change into their nightclothes and be part of the fun, but then be picked up to go home at, for instance, 10.30pm.

▶ Encourage children to bring not just their night comforter, such as a blanket or teddy bear, but their own pillow, which will smell familiar – smell is a particularly evocative sense.

▶ Have the home and mobile phone numbers of the parents of all the children who are staying over, and make it clear you will phone them if necessary and have the right to expect someone to collect their child if need be: it is only fair on everybody else.

Be prepared for times when all is not as calm and peaceful as in this picture.

2 Party themes

Having a party theme helps you to make decisions about decorations, games and food. It provides a focus for the event and should stimulate a few creative ideas about ways to make the party fun. This section aims to help you choose a theme that will suit your child and gives advice on how to work to that theme. Flexibility is the key word here, however: stay in charge of that party and don't let the theme take over!

The hook

A theme can bring a party alive. It is a 'hook' on which you can hang ideas for games, foods, decorations, party bags and clothes. Children love playing with ideas and will enjoy working the party theme into the party themselves.

Choosing a theme

Much of the fun of a party lies in the planning and anticipation, and choosing a theme is a major part of that. Your child may have an idea of a theme that appeals to her, and this can be as wacky as she likes – themes are usually very adaptable. Some ideas to start you off are:

► A favourite toy, like a rocket.

► Special clothing – maybe your child loves to dress up and has a new outfit.

► Hobbies such as sports or playing an instrument.

► A book your child loves, whether it be fiction (you could use the location, or the characters) or information (the topic becomes the theme).

► A favourite television programme or song.

► If you know you want to book an entertainer, that could set the theme. So booking a conjuror could mean you'll have a 'magic' party.

► If you have chosen a party venue such as a swimming pool or bowling alley, that could set the theme.

► Most party goods suppliers have websites that list what they offer for a variety of themes (page 188).

► Visit a shop that sells party goods and see what appeals to your child – you don't have to buy everything related to the theme, just use the idea.

► The birthday may be at a time of year that links with an obvious theme, such as Halloween or Christmas.

► There may be a new children's film that is all the rage that you could tie the party in with.

This chapter includes advice on using 20 of the most popular current party themes and which can also be adapted to suit your own child.

Developing ideas

No theme is too ambitious, because you can simplify it and adapt it according to what is possible. However, the key is to exploit it as much as you can. Each theme featured over the following pages has suggestions for how to tie in:

▶ Invitations
▶ Decorations
▶ Clothes
▶ Face paint
▶ A birthday cake

▶ Food
▶ Games
▶ Prizes
▶ Party bags

You probably won't want to do something in every category, but you will get a sense of what you like and what is possible. If you start thinking about this early enough, you'll have lots of ideas of things that would be fun to do that match the theme.

Many children adore dressing up to match a party theme.

Action hero

Is it a bird? Is it a plane? No, it's a superhero with special powers, a mask and cape, and the ability to make merry quips while vanquishing the baddies. Action heroes are enduringly popular with children and are a smash hit at parties.

A mask and a cape is all it takes to transform a child into a superhero!

Invitations

A card with the action hero's picture or logo on it, or just the attention-grabbing word 'Pow!' mounted onto card will communicate the theme. Alternatively, you could stick a speech bubble with the invitee's name next to a picture of the superhero.

Decorations

Display pictures and posters if you have them (try your local cinema – they may even have an old cardboard cut-out). Use comic books as place mats, and populate the table with action figures.

Clothes and face paint

Guests could dress as superheroes. When they arrive, you could give them a mask or create one with face paint (page 33). You could use old, spare bits of fabric as capes that carry special powers.

Food and the cake

Create some 'baddies' by making animals or aliens out of rolls and cocktail sticks or toothpicks (page 147). For the birthday cake, decorate a tray-bake cake (page 165) with a logo or mask symbol using icing – you could do the same on biscuits and small cakes, too.

Games

Have a scavenger hunt to find a collection of hidden objects, but for the party call it a Special mission. Adapt Cops and robbers (page 98) to Heroes and villains. Play Hit the target (page 101) as if the superhero is trying to zap the baddies.

Prizes and party bags

Plastic superhero figures and comic books featuring them will go down well. If you got hold of some posters or stand-up cut-outs, they could become prizes and save you the trouble of removing the decorations! You could make badges saying 'superhero' and issue them to winners of games or those who have tried hard.

Bugs

Many children are fascinated by insects and will happily study their movements and actions for hours. Others, of course, find them pretty scary, so check if this is the case with anybody on the guest list. Bugs can be pretty and harmless (like butterflies) or ugly and aggressive (like wasps), so their appeal is wide ranging!

watch out!

Choking
Remember that small plastic toys can be a choking hazard for young children.

Invitations

Use green as your base colour, drawing on a few lines for veins. You could cut the card to an insect shape or decorate it with beetle prints. Buy some small plastic bugs or make them from card and put a few in the envelope so they spill out when opened.

Decorations

Decorate the walls with giant leaves made from green crêpe paper. Hang plastic bugs and spiders from the ceilings and doorways. To create a jungle effect, tape streamers so they hang down like vines, and glue or tape a few bugs to some of them. Use black wool to create a giant spider's web in one corner.

Clothes and face paint

Headbands can be adapted to have little antennae sticking up and wings are always fun to add – perhaps you can adapt a set of fairy wings, which are readily available from toy shops .

Food and the cake

Join slabs of cake to create an even or bumpy surface and cover it with green icing to make a grassy background for some plastic bugs. Create realistic grass with dessicated coconut dyed green. Make a marshy dip using mashed avocado, with long antennae made from finely sliced carrots to dip into it. You can turn rolls or baguettes into 'bugs' by attaching olives or blueberries using

cocktail sticks or toothpicks. Follow that with butterfly cakes (see Queen cakes, page 158), or make some bug-type sweets with marshmallows as the bodies decorated with icing and with chocolate matchstick or liquorice legs.

You can turn Queen cakes (page 158) into butterfly cakes and make them as multicoloured as you like. Sticks of angelica with mini chocolate drops stuck on the ends make perfect antennae.

Games
Adapt Sleeping lions (page 99) to Sleeping bugs; get the children to draw insects in Blind drawing (page 112), and re-name Chain race (page 132) as the Caterpillar race.

Prizes and party bags
There are plenty of plastic bugs, and bug-shaped sweets. Look out for worm- or snake-shaped lollies and liquorice. A magnifying lens for insect-studying makes an enviable prize.

Circus

A circus or carnival theme immediately creates a sense of fun and adventure at a party. As host, you are transformed into the ringmaster, welcoming the audience into the Big Top.

Invitations

Use balloon or clown shapes to decorate the Party card on page 72, or add a large clown face design. Or use a computer to create a printed 'ticket' to the circus party.

Decorations

Hang streamers from a central point in the room, fanning them out to create a Big Top effect. The clowns in your family will be delighted to place a whoopie cushion on each seat at the food table. There are plenty of circus-themed plates, bowls and napkins available from tableware suppliers, too.

Clothes and face paint

Feeling brave? Hire or make some clown, ringmaster or strong-man outfits. If that is going a step too far, restrict yourself to face painting clown faces (or just a red nose) and some twirly strong-man moustaches.

Food and the cake

It is fairly straightforward to create a circle from a Tray-bake cake (page 165), which you can ice into a clown face. Bowls of popcorn and sticks of candy floss fit the theme perfectly.

Games

Packet pickup (page 110) requires the grace and balance of a trapeze artist. Adapt Flap the kipper (page 127) by making a huge shoe shape and flapping it across the circus ring.

A simple prop like this fake weightlifting bar can inspire a game: who can lift if with the most realistically huge effort?

Prizes and party bags

Popcorn is a suitable edible prize, but you could also give out joke books for those aspiring clowns, juggling balls or plastic figures of circus animals.

Colours

Everybody has a favourite colour, and children love playing with colours and seeing how different mixes turn out. Colour is a versatile party theme because the host and guest can take on as much or as little as they like and still make a contribution.

Invitations

See the Colour card on page 74 for a simple and stylish rendering of the theme. Punch out paper or card holes to make coloured confetti and drop a handful into the envelope before you seal it, so it will cascade out when the invitation is opened.

There is a huge choice of coloured tableware and crockery: mix and match or go for a two-colour theme.

Decorations

Make your home or party room a multicoloured

festival with streamers and balloons. Make simple decorative flower shapes out of coloured pipe cleaners and use them as a table centrepiece. Put out a plain white paper tablecloth and let the guests decorate it with felt tip pens (page 84). Make a mural by giving each child one colour and getting him to add designs to a large banner of plain paper.

Clothes and face paint

Ask guests to wear as many colours as they can, or give each one a different colour. As they arrive, paint their noses and cheeks in bright, primary colours or to match the clothes that they're wearing.

Food and the cake

Food dye can transform the plainest sandwich into something strange and exotic. See how many colours you can include in a pizza topping, for instance. Use strips of coloured icing to make a multicoloured cake. Frosted fruits (page 162) are suitably colourful, as is layered jelly (page 161).

Games

Use coloured balloons for a variety of games (pages 100–105). Adapt Ticket man (page 111) using colours instead of place names and use dyed water for How much did you spill? (page 123). Play Wear the lot race (page 125) with clothes of the same colour for each team. Use colours to identify the teams.

Prizes and party bags

Art supplies, such as colouring pens and crayons and stickers, are always welcome. For bigger prizes, consider colouring books or even a water colour set.

Cowboys and Indians

Set your party in the Wild West, where the sheriff keeps a beady eye on proceedings and every game starts with a cry of 'Yee ha!' This theme lends itself particularly well to adapting games for it.

Invitations
Make a simply decorated Party card (page 72) and hole punch some 'bullet holes' into it. Or go for a printed poster format and head it 'Wanted: party guests'. There is also a good choice of cowboy and Indian rubber stamps.

Decorations
Turn the kitchen into a saloon bar by strewing a little straw or sawdust onto the floor and play country and western music. Make a few 'Wanted' posters, perhaps featuring your guests, and hang some lassoes on the wall.

Clothes
Jeans and a waistcoat create the cowboy look, with a Stetson hat if possible. Checked bandanas and/or neckerchiefs also bring a touch of the Wild West.

Food and the cake
Cut a Tray-bake cake (page 165) into the shape of a sheriff's star. Serve 'branded' potatoes where you carve initials into the vegetable before baking it. Sausage and beans were popular fare around the camp fire, preferably served on a tin plate.

Games
Adapt any version of tag, or Cops and robbers (page 98) into Cowboys and Indians. Hot potato (page 109) sounds authentically Wild West, and you could always have a water pistol duel.

Prizes and party bags
Go for belt buckles and plastic cowboy and Indian figures.

The rough and ready Wild West theme can suit both boys and girls and is ideal for games. Squaw outfits look great with tassls or unevenly cut hems, and a feather finishes off a headband nicely. Any self-respecting Indian would have face-painted strips on her cheeks.

Crafts

Most children enjoy practical activities where they make and take home something, and craft parties are increasingly widespread, with card making being one of the most popular. Go for something you are confident about or happy to experiment with, or find an expert helper – maybe a local supplier.

Children love practical activities, especially when they get to take the results home. Show them one or two simple techniques and then leave them to the fun of putting them into practice.

Invitations

Your invitation can show how a sophisticated effect can be achieved with time and patience – try the shoes and bags or Pink fairy cards on pages 76 and 77. Or send a very plain card with a message saying, 'Learn how to make this card more interesting!'

Decorations

Set up a display of the materials, scissors and glue that will be available during the party. Stamp or paint repeating patterns onto large sheets of paper and hang them on the walls.

Clothes

Dressing up isn't required for this kind of party, but do have aprons (or ask guests to bring these) on hand to protect valued clothes from scissors and glue.

Food and the cake

As the accent is on being practical and making things, set up a 'fill-your-own' roll or sandwich bar or let children decorate their own pizzas (page 153). Put out icing equipment so that children can decorate small cakes or biscuits. Maybe they could cook them too?

Games

Try drawing games such as Blind drawing (page 112) and Drawing consequences (page 113). A fun game for any young artist is 'bagface', where players put a paper bag over their head and try to draw their face on the outside. Move on from games to activities such as decorating plain T-shirts using fabric pens.

Prizes and party bags

Make up packs of biscuits (page 159) that have been made and decorated at the party, putting them in an attractive bag or box (page 89). Other prizes could include small pieces of craft equipment, pens and stickers, and maybe a voucher for materials from a local craft shop.

must know

Crafty ideas
There are plenty of options other than card making for a crfat party. Ideas include jewellery making with beads, badge making, sculpting with salt dough, cooking or paitning (try using watercolours and/or oil pastels for variety).

Dinosaurs

Many a young chap (and a few girls) is obsessed with dinosaurs, and part of their appeal as a party theme is finding ways to tie in everything – food, clothes, games – with pre-historic times. Cave dwellers may not be historically accurate, but it adds to the fun!

Invitations
Use dinosaur stamps to decorate the cards on pages 74 or 76. Or write the invitation on a piece of paper and conceal it inside a plastic egg. Deliver the 'dino egg' and await the the cavemen!

Decorations
Decorate the room with large-scale dinosaur prints cut out of paper. Hang sheets from the wall or ceiling to create a 'cave'.

Clothes and face paint
Paint scales on cheeks to look like dinosaur skin, or blacken eyes to give that hollow-cheeked caveman look.

Food and the cake
See page 155 for Potato shapes, made with cutters that could also be used to create biscuits and sandwiches. Serve chicken (dino) legs and spare ribs (page 151). Decorate a cake with icing in a dino footprint shape; add spikes with chocolate matchsticks.

Games
Have a scavenger hunt for dino eggs. Play Stepping stones (page 131) but use dinosaur prints. Play tag: herbivores vs carnivores.

A dinosaur piñata matches the theme and is a fine excuse for caveman aggression.

Prizes and party bags
Small plastic dinosaur models fit the bill, and have a large inflatable one as a main prize.

Fairies

In the world of the fairies, people make friends with elves and pixies, play games and create a little mischief. Sounds a bit like a children's party, doesn't it? For some girls, a fairy party is heaven. Don't forget to get everybody to clap to show they believe in fairies!

Invitations

The Pink fairy card on page 77 obviously fits the bill, but there are plenty of fairy stamps if you prefer the style of the shoes and bags card on page 76. Pop a spoonful of glitter into the card so that whoever opens it finds a little shower of 'fairy dust'.

Decorations

Cut out butterflies and flowers in pastel shades and create a soft backdrop for these gentle creatures by hanging lengths of fabric on the walls. Dig out the Christmas lights and use them to illuminate fairyland.

Clothes and face paint

Make fairy wands with canes covered in foil or pink paper. Paint flowers and butterflies on cheeks – and few fairies turn down the chance of some glittery eyeshade or lipstick.

Food and the cake

Cut sandwiches and biscuits in butterfly shapes like fairy wings, plus have some wraps, cheese straws or Sugared bread fingers (pages 147–9) to make edible wands. Re-name Queen cakes (page 158) as Fairy wing cakes. Use fairy magic with jelly (see page 161 for ideas). Draw happy faces on biscuits (page 159).

Games

Try Hide the fairy (page 108) or the Coat game (page 107).

Prizes and party bags

Little fairies love glitter and nail varnish. Small bags of sweets tied with a ribbon can be fairy gifts. Any pink glittery pencils, sharpeners or erasers will be welcome in fairyland.

Wings, wand, a sparkly dress: what six-year-old girl could want more?

Fashion doll

Fashion dolls remain among the most popular toys for young girls, and they love playing the part of their miniature heroines. Think pink and pretty and you've got a party theme! Ask your guests to bring along their favourite doll for a catwalk parade.

Invitations

With its high visual interest and choice of colour and fabric, the Pink fairy card on page 77 is perfect for fashion doll parties. Or cut out pictures of fashion dolls and stick on speech bubbles with the invitee's name.

This layered pink and red jelly is fit for a princess - and her fashion doll.

Decorations

Put out all the fashion dolls in the house next to pretty boxes of accessories and you probably won't need to worry about party games. Hang pink or sparkly fabrics as a glamorous backdrop. A table centrepiece of fashion dolls will match your theme perfectly.

Clothes and face paint

Invite guests to come dressed as a fashion doll. Have plenty of necklaces, rings, bracelets and clip-on earrings handy so they can accessorize. You could have a 'nail bar' or 'make-up bar' where guests can add a few touches to their look.

Food and the cake

Elegant ringed fingers should hold the Sugared bread fingers (page 149) and Frosted fruits (page 162). Make necklaces from pretty pink and white sweets - they'll be a good prize and party bag item too. In addition to the layered jelly pictured left (use fromage frais rather than water for the middle layer), see other jelly ideas on page 160.

Games

This is a dressing-up party, so the Wear the lot race (page 125) and Dressing-up relay (page 133) or Dress me up! (page 127) are ideal. Change Happy birthday your majesty (page 137) so that children address the fashion doll by name. Test guests' knowledge of their doll with the Twenty-second list (page 139), before holding a Talent show (page 119).

Prizes and party bags

Fashion doll accessories are the obvious choice here, but any 'girly' stationery items such as pencils, sharpeners and erasers will be fine. Rings, bracelets and necklaces will be popular. Glittery bendy straws are ideal for the cocktail-sipping girl about town. For reading matter, go for girly magazines.

Film

In these days of videos and DVDs, kids are familiar with a huge range of films and film characters, so you can select from the back catalogue or try to tie in with the latest blockbuster. Either way, the party has the red-carpet style of a Hollywood premiere.

Invitations

Adapt the cards on pages 74 or 76, adding plenty of glitzy glitter. If the favoured film is a Bond-style spy movie, write the invitation in milk – it is invisible until heated in the oven (include the instructions and a reminder to get an adult to help).

Decorations

You might be able to get posters or even cardboard cut-outs promoting the movie. Go for a film-set look with director's chairs and 'Quiet please, filming in progress' signs under a red light bulb. Keep a movie themes CD playing in the background.

Clothes and face paint

Cool shades are compulsory for film stars and after that it is just cooly elegant glamour, or an outfit from the film. Fancy dress shops always have outfits from popular kids' films.

Food and the cake

There may be a commercially made cake tying in with the film, or spell out its title in edible letters. Movie food includes hot dogs and popcorn, but also go for glitzy premier fare such as Pinwheels (page 147) and Frosted fruits (page 162).

Games

Try acting games such as Living mirror (page 98), Charades (page 97) and, for dialogue, Chinese whispers (page 136).

Children love dressing up in outfits from classic and contemporary movies.

Prizes and party bags

Cool film-star shades are a welcome addition to any child's wardrobe. You could also give your guests small bags of popcorn to enjoy during the next blockbuster and maybe vouchers for the local cinema.

Halloween

With its mix of ghouls and witches, gore and mischief, Halloween appeals to many children and is one of the easiest party themes to work with. Be aware that some children can get seriously spooked by the dark and talk of ghosts, so keep the tone jokey.

Scary, isn't she? Witches are easy to spot at Halloween.

Invitations

There are plenty of commercially made Halloween invitations in the shops, but really a blend of blood-red writing and black bat stamps or stickers will do the job admirably. Pop in a few small plastic bugs or spiders so they fall out of the envelope and surprise the recipient. That should set the mood. It might be fun to include a 'Halloween' secret password with which your guests can gain entry.

Decorations

Dim the lights, put black paper over the windows, hang plastic bats and woollen cobwebs from the doors and you've got a truly spooky setting.

Clothes and face paint

Apply some glow-in-the-dark stickers to faces and clothing as people arrive and they'll enjoy the spooky dark interior.

Food and the cake

Dye food such as sandwiches and cakes red, with added gore supplied by tomato ketchup. Wrap some ghoulish plastic figures in cling film and hide them in the cooked cake to give everybody a nasty shock (but beware of the choking hazard). Dead man's fingers (page 163) are a must, or try the vegetable version (page 155). Follow these with frothy-top jelly (page 161) or just chop up red jelly and call it 'blood and guts'.

Games

Traditional Halloween games include apple bobbing and eating a doughnut off a string. Act a gory story in Act the tale (page 96), and change Frozen laugh (page 98) to a scream. Try also Make a face (page 102) or change Grandmother's footsteps (page 122) into Witch's steps, and turn the fish into a cat for Flap the kipper (page 127) – the newspaper is a wand.

Prizes and party bags

Wands, snakes, liquorice worms, false long fingernails will all match the theme. Keep guests safe with a lucky rabbit's foot.

Pirates

Just the right side of scary, pirates are rough and ready and carry swords and a hook, but are also togged out in rather dandyish lacy and flouncy outfits that suggest a hidden, softer side. The pirate theme suits both boys and girls, so might be a good idea for a mixed-sex party.

Invitations

Draw a 'treasure map' with your house marked with a cross, stain it by rubbing it with a used tea bag, and when the paper dries, roll it into a scroll. Every buccaneer in the playground will be hugely impressed and, even better, enjoy finding their way to the hidden treasure on the day itself!

Decorations

Take your pick from a wide variety of props that are available: stuffed parrots, cardboard skeletons or crossbones, skulls, anchors, inflatable palm trees and treasure maps.

Clothes and face paint

Give every guest an eye patch on their arrival. Stripy shirts, three-quarter-length trousers and bare feet is the look for the deck, set off with a bandana. Press-on tattoos and clip-on earrings finish the effect.

Food and the cake

Go for a plain Tray-bake cake (page 165) covered in ready-made black icing with a skull and crossbones drawn with an icing pen. Filo pastry can be made into 'bags of gold' (page 148). Chicken drumsticks and spare ribs (pages 150 and 151) will furnish a ready supply of bones, and should be served with plenty of that goriest of sauces – tomato ketchup.

Games

Adapt Hit the target (page 101) to Hit the captain, while Grandmother's footsteps (page 122) could easily be Crocodile steps. The Treasure hunt (page 131) is a must, and the inevitable pirate fight can take place as Below the knee (with a soft 'cannonball') on page 132.

A couple of very scary hearties looking very cheerful despite their various disabilities.

Prizes and party bags

Every landlubber should leave wearing an eye patch and clutching a bag of gold (coins). Other gifts could include a bandana, telescope and a sheet of tattoos.

Princesses

Of course any birthday girl is princess for the day, and her guests will enjoy being part of the regal birthday court. This is a chance to go completely over the top with dresses and accessories.

Invitations

The Shoes and bags card on page 76 could be adapted with crown and tiara stamps. Alternatively, opt for heavy card with flowery gold lettering, or a royal scroll tied with a red ribbon.

Decorations

Hang a bead curtains in the doorway to announce each royal entrance. Display a family coat of arms and hang red velvet for that medieval-castle look. Sprinkle sequins and plastic jewels over the food table.

Clothes and face paint

A royal dress with puffed-up sleeves and jewel-encrusted top is a must, accessorized by rings, necklace and a tiara. No self-respecting princess has less than perfectly painted nails.

Food and the cake

Ice cream cones make great castle turrets for your palace cake, while you can ice in the window and door frames. Princesses like delicate foods such as Chocolate fruit (page 162). Thread sweets onto cotton to make edible necklaces.

Games

Test out regal ears with Happy Birthday your majesty (page 137), followed by a right royal Treasure hunt (page 131) around the palace and making a royal necklace in the Paperclip race (page 129). Act the tale (page 96) could include a more genteel story involving kings and queens. Test out royal balancing skills with Packet pickup (page 110) and re-christen New planet (page 113) as New kingdom.

Prizes and party bags

'Girly' stationery and make-up items will bring a smile to the face of most princesses.

Every birthday girl is princess for the day.

Robots

Ask children to move in the manner of something else and some of them are sure to start strutting about like a robot. The idea of an expressionless automaton with jerky limbs and a monotonous voice just seems to appeal.

Invitations

Use squares and rectangles to create a robot shape, as in the picture below. Get the metal look with silver card and use a silver pen to write the message. Print the invitation text from the computer in capitals to give it a rigid, uniform look.

This robot card is simple and fun to create – get your child to run some off!

Decorations

Sheets of tin foil create a metallic backdrop. Make robot heads out of cardboard boxes and display them or let children wear them if they are the leader in a game (who should, of course, be known as the lead robot).

Clothes and face paint

Grey or silver faces will be robot-like, if slightly off-putting at the food table. Children could try using cardboard boxes as robot heads or cardboard tubes as robot arms. Split pins would make very good 'rivets'.

Food and the cake

Create a robot face by baking a square Tray-bake cake (page 165) or use slabs or cake, then make the mouth and eyes using rows of silver balls. Make a robot face in a dipping sauce (see page 156), then roll out pizza dough into a square and decorate your own robot pizza (page 152). Make more robot shapes with fruits (see box, page 163) and decorate cakes and biscuits with square-featured faces (page 159).

Games

Grandmother's footsteps (page 122) can be adapted into Robot footsteps. Who swapped? (page 111) can be played using numbers and letters for the 'robots'. Change the Baby race (page 120) into Feed the robot. Simon says (page 138) can transform into the Robot says.

Prizes and party bags

Anything metallic such as silver pencils and sharpeners fits the theme, as do transformer and mechanical wind-up toys. A plastic kazoo musical instrument turns sounds into buzzing noises, which could the be put to good use as a robot orchestra playing a robot symphony.

Space

Outer space is thrillingly remote yet visible, and children love the idea of space travel in rockets to strange planets full of aliens. So space appeals to the storyteller in all of us, and makes a very popular party theme.

Invitations

Adapt the robot card (page 52) or the Football card (page 73) to feature images of astronauts. Or print a ticket to outer space on a rocket-shaped piece of card. Use black paper backgrounds and a silver pen for 'moon writing'.

Decorations

Dim the lights and darken the windows with black paper studded with glow-in-the-dark stars. Dig out the Christmas tree lights to become the flickering control panel of a space ship. On the food table use foil mats and have place cards written with 'Planet (name)'.

Clothes and face paint

A rucksack makes a pretty good rocketpack for a little astronaut – you might even consider covering it in silver foil – and you could ask your guests to wear oven mitts as space gloves.

Food and the cake

Make the cake (page 165) in a circle or crescent shape, cover with white icing and silver balls and it becomes a moon cake. Mashed avocado makes an excellent 'Alien dip', followed by 'potato meterorites' (baked potatoes in foil, with cocktails sticks for that satellite look). Sausages, ribs and kebabs (page 151) are all fairly rocket-shaped, and you could cut potatoes or biscuits into star and moon shapes (pages 155 and 159).

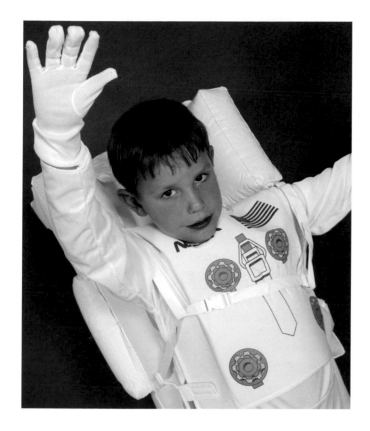

Moonwalk to the party
in an astronaut suit.

Games

Change Hit the target (page 101) into Rocket launch. Ticket
man (page 111) can have a space theme, while Hot potato
(page 109) becomes Pass the meterorite. See also New planet
(page 113) and the Broom game (page 121), which could be a
space walk.

Prizes and party bags

Plastic alien figures are always popular and collectible items,
especially if they are squishy. Glow-in-the-dark stickers and
even posters or small books about space and the planets will
go down well, too.

Sports

Sports parties are ideal for lively, energetic children who get fidgety when asked to sit, listen and talk, write or draw. You need a suitable space – outdoors or a village hall – and to be prepared for competitive natures to express themselves.

Invitations

The Football card on page 73 will work well, or go for a simpler design like the party card on page 72, using sports stamps or stickers. For something more unusual, how about sending the invite in the form of a certificate or even a medal?

Sports parties can appeal to girls every bit as much as ultra-competitive boys.

Decorations

Decorate the room with pennants and flags, maybe even hoops and frisbees (either accept they'll be removed and played with or secure them very firmly). A green tablecloth will set a sporty theme on the food table, with plastic sports figures as a centrepiece or scattered over the table. Watch out for choking hazards (if the children are very young).

Clothes and face paint

The children will be playing active games so get them to wear sports gear. You might want to provide bibs or sashes for team games, or perhaps a blob of face paint will be sufficient to identify each group.

Food and the cake

The cake could be slabs (page 165) cut into an oval or figure of eight to make a running or race track, and covered with green icing. Serve lots of circle-shaped foods such as Pinwheels (page 147) and Shaped mash (page 154). Adapt the idea on page 152 for soccer or sports pizzas. Sports stars need to stay healthy, so check out the fruit options on page 163.

Games

See Hockey (page 102), Penalty! (page 104), Shot put and Volleyball (page 105). You could try Bucket goal (page 121) and, for large groups, French cricket (page 122) and Kick bowling (page 124).

Prizes and party bags

Sporty items such as whistles and soft or rubber balls will appeal. You could give out plastic trophies or gold-foiled wrapped chocolate 'medals'.

Must know

Winning parties
Sports parties are bound to encourage competition, which can provoke ultra-competitive behaviour somewhat against the party spirit. Keep mixing up teams and keep the tone as light-hearted as possible. Award prizes for effort and cheerfulness rather than for being first.

Teddy bears

Nearly every young child has a teddy bear, and some remain very attached to their furry chums for years. Teddy parties are particularly good for shy youngsters as they can keep their familiar, reassuring 'friend' with them throughout the event.

Invitations
Use teddy stamps and stickers to adapt the cards on pages 72 or 76. Alternatively, cut a teddy bear shape out of card, get your child to colour the front, and put the message on the back.

Decorations
A check tablecloth is ideal for a teddy bears' picnic, but any rug or simple cloth will do. Teddy-shaped place cards will add to the fun, as will as many teddy bears as you can gather together.

Clothes and face paint
A brown or black spot of face paint on the nose suggests a bear. Steer clear of bear outfits: they are incredibly hot.

Food and the cake
Cut a teddy shape out of cake slabs (page 165), using chocolate sprinkles or shredded coconut for fur, cup cakes for ears and chocolate buttons for the face). Teddy-shaped cutters will create sandwiches (honey, obviously) and biscuits to match.

Games
Little bears like circle games and singalongs (pages 106 and 118).

Prizes and party bags
Mini teddies will suit your guests, or give hats and other clothing their furry friends can wear.

All is well when teddy comes too.

Trains and transport

Trains, planes and automobiles have a magnetic attraction for some children. Any one of these makes a fine party theme because they can be used in games, clothing and food – and the party bags are very straightforward!

Invitations

Use the basic Party card design on page 72 but add transport-themed stickers or stamps. Or get on the computer and create a party ticket with arrival and departure times.

Decorations

Draw a train track or road system onto a blank paper tablecloth and watch the children push their vehicles around on it. You could arrange the seats in rows as if they were on a train or plane.

Clothes

A railway worker's hat and whistle might be fun to give to game leaders.

Food and the cake

There are plenty of commercially made train and car cakes on the market. You can stick together cakes of different shapes and sizes (page 165) to make pretty reasonable birthday cakes of your own, too. Make Pinwheels (page 147), which resemble train wheels, or cut sandwiches and Biscuits (page 159) in wheel or simple train shapes. Both Shaped mash (page 154) and frothy-top jelly (page 161) look like smoke coming out of a train funnel.

Games

Change Where am I going? (page 140) into Guide the driver. Try Wacky races (page 135) where children have to move similar vehicles, and the Chain race (page 132) converts into the Train race faster than you can say, 'Train track!' Jacket race (page 128) can become Driver uniform race, while Flap the kipper (page 127) is easily adapted into Flap the train.

Prizes and party bags

Plastic or metal model cars or other vehicles will be very much welcomed by this audience. They might also enjoy being given a miniature compass to help find their way home.

Save yourself the trouble and buy a ready-made train-themed cake – you can still add your own decorations to make it a little more personal.

Tropical

The tropical party theme has become especially popular with young and pre-teenage girls. Stick colourful decorations on the walls, turn up the heating, put on the Hawaiian CD and soak up the fun!

Aloha! There is a lot of scope for decorations and clothing to match the tropical theme.

Invitations

See the Tropical card on page 75 for an effective and surprisingly simple. Alternatives might be to use a ticket format with arrival and departure times, or write the invitation in the form of a holiday postcard from a tropical destination.

Decorations

Inflatable or extendible palm trees are widely available (use a small one as a table centrepiece). Cut out large green paper leaves to serve as decorations or place mats, and cut large, colourful flower shapes out of crêpe paper. Door curtains with hanging plastic flowers make a great backdrop.

Clothes

Sunglasses are essential, and you could make a simple grass skirt out of crêpe paper or rafia for each guest to put on over swimwear. Flower necklaces and accessories complete the effect.

Food and the cake

Adapt the centrepiece idea on page 86 to make a tasty tropical delight. Use a tray-bake cake (page 165) and really go over the top with the decorations. Top almost any food with pineapple and it has a tropical flavour. Add it to cream cheese to make a tropical dip, then put pieces on top of a pizza (page 152) to make a Hawaiian surprise. Serve jelly (page 160) in scooped-out orange or grapefruit fruit 'bowls'. Make shapes with tropical fruits or use it to make Fresh fruit kebabs (page 163) or Fruit dips (page 157).

Games

Sunburst (page 105) is a good game for sunny weather, and Packet pickup (page 110) will be an excellent warm-up for limbo dancing. The tropical theme suits water games (there are two on page 124) and the Orange race (page 129).

Prizes and party bags

Give out shades, sun visors, fans or a beach ball.

Zoo

The zoo theme gives you licence to include any animal, including farmyard ones. It lends itself very well to games and decorations, and is likely to appeal to many children as just about every child has a favourite animal.

Invitations

Adapt the Tropical card on page 75 to make a simple animal habitat, or use the Party card format on page 72, incorporating animal stamps or stickers.

Decorations

Make cages or just bars from cardboard and populate them with card or stuffed animals. Paint cages or pens onto a blank white tablecloth (page 84) and let the children draw their own animals.

Clothes and face paint

This party theme is crying out for children to have their faces painted in various animal guises. Get one or two helpers to do this job for you, capturing each guest as they arrive.

Food and the cake

Decorate a round cake like a face with whiskers and use cup cakes for ears. Cut sandwiches or biscuits in the shape of animals or claws and make Potato shapes (page 155). Create animal face pizzas (page 152) and biscuits (page 159), and you can also make faces in dipping sauces (page 156 and box). Serve 'monkey food' (chopped fruit).

Games

Play 'animal bingo' where children draw animals on their card and you then call a series of beasts until someone has the lot.

Try also the Zoo game and Sleeping lions on page 99, or turn the Chain race (page 132) into a Snake race.

Prizes and party bags

Toy plastic animals would be great in party bags (but beware potential choking harard with young children), but you can also buy soft toy animals quite cheaply, for a special gift.

Children can meet real animals as part of a magic show, too.

3 Invitations

Buying invitations and then sending them out is an exciting part of organizing a party. Making them is even better. This section has plenty of advice on how to create your own invitations and six 'start you off' ideas for different cards that can be adapted to your theme. It can be really satisfying making your own cards with your child – just make sure you remember to put the key 'when and where' information in there, too!

Come to my party

Making your own party invitations can be great fun and incredibly satisfying. With a few simple materials, you can create your own personal message that matches your theme and reflects you and your child's personalities.

Starting out

Even if you haven't made cards before, you can produce simple, personal invitations easily, given time and patience. Your cards will match your party theme perfectly, and you can work with your child on making them, adding to the fun of preparing for the party. The invitations do not have to be identical, so you can enjoy experimenting with different ideas for each one.

There is a wide variety of decorations that you can buy to adorn your cards.

Tools

These basic stationery items will be useful:

Craft knife: Good for cutting curves.

Cutting mat: Protects your table. Alternatively, you can use layers of newspaper or a sheet of thick cardboard.

Paper trimmer: Allows you to make quick, clean, straight and accurate cuts far more easily than with scissors.

Rulers: Plastic for measuring, metal to cut along.

Scissors: Large for cutting different materials; small for cutting details; decorative-edging scissors for a range of finishes on edges, such as waves and scallop shapes.

Materials

Paper and card: There is a huge selection of hand- and machine-made card and paper. It comes in a variety of finishes such as matt, glossy, metallic and corrugated. If you don't have a trimmer, buy the smaller A4 and A5 sizes.

▶ Hand-made paper usually has a rough texture and can feature flower petals, leaves, wood and metallic flecks held within the paper. It is more expensive than other types of paper.

▶ Mulberry paper is light, opaque and made from mulberry leaves. It comes in many colours and when damp will tear with a feathered edge.

▶ Patterned paper is useful for backgrounds or to cut motifs from.

▶ Vellum is semi-opaque and can be plain or patterned. It is used for layering.

Adhesives: There is a wide range available and with many purposes. Use solvent-based glues in

did you know?

More specialist tools

▶ Decorative punches: For making holes in various designs and sizes – useful for producing identical decorative shapes like stars

▶ Rubber stamps: With decorations or messages. This are a good investment if you are going to make lots of cards.

▶ Bone folder: For scoring card if you are making your own blanks.

must know

What, when, where and who?

If you are making your own invitations, it is very easy to forget basic essential information. Depending on the style of card, it may be best to print these details onto paper and stick them inside the card or on the reverse so that you know everyone has the right information. Your invitation should include:

▶ Who it is from
▶ Your address
▶ The venue for the party (if it is not at your house)
▶ A map showing how to get to the party (if necessary)
▶ The theme and if children should wear special clothes
▶ The date plus the start and finish times of the party
▶ The date by which people should reply (RSVP)

well-ventilated conditions and do not let children usse them .

▶ PVA glue sticks paper and card and dries clear.
▶ Gluesticks are useful for thinner materials such as mulberry paper.
▶ Spray adhesive allows you to glue thin papers without them wrinkling.
▶ Glue pens are for attaching small items to card.
▶ Glitter glue applies a decorative glittery finish.
▶ Glue dots are for attaching small items to cards.
▶ Adhesive tape and double-sided tape will hold heavier materials such as card.
▶ Foam pads and 3-D tape allows you to place a raised picture or embellishment so it stands out.

   Writing and decorating: It is useful to have a range of pens, pencils and paints:
▶ Felt tip pens are for colouring and writing messages as well as inking rubber stamps.
▶ Gel pens.
▶ Silver and gold marker pens are particularly effective to make words stand out.
▶ Watercolour, metallic and 3-D paints.
▶ Inkpads for colouring rubber stamps.
▶ Buttons, beads, glitter, gems, stickers, brads (which are coloured split pins) and ribbons can be used for embellishments.

Card shapes and styles

There is no limit to the style and shape of your invitation card. Look at the ideas on the following pages and at cards in shops. You can fold your own card or buy ready-scored and folded blanks in card and craft shops. The photograph opposite shows the most straightforward of shapes and those that are most readily available. You might otherwise choose to use just a single piece of unfolded card with the important details written on the front.

A simple start

If you are just starting out, it makes sense to go for a simple design. If you can't find one you like, experiment by folding A4 paper in different ways. Be aware that if you make the card yourself, you will need to measure, cut, score and fold it, and if it is not a standard size, you might need a larger envelope.

Some examples of card shapes are listed below. Each shape can feature a cut-out:

▶ Single-fold cards, which can be any shape or size. The outer flap can be narrower than the base flap (see page 77).

▶ Concertina cards have three panels, which will all be visible on the finished card.

▶ Aperture cards have three panels, one of which is folded in.

▶ Gatefold cards open out like a pair of gates.

Cut the workload by using coloured card so the background is taken care of. Here are examples of simple folds to vary the look of your invitations.

Six starting points

These pages feature six card designs, which use several simple techniques such as layering, stamping and adding stickers for creating a professional-looking card. The ideas could be adapted to any party theme with a little imagination and, possibly, the right rubber stamp. All these cards are made using card blanks.

Party card

This is a general-purpose, un-themed party card, which could be made to match your theme if you used different stickers. The wavy line on the white card is produced using decorative-edging scissors.

Making the card

1 Cut the white card to 7 x 11.5cm (2³/₄ x 4¹/₂in) and trim with decorative-edging scissors.
2 Layer this card onto the red and then purple card, leaving small borders.
3 Apply the stickers and message strip from an off-cut of the white card.
4 Decorate with glitter glue and mount onto the card blank.

You will need
White, red and purple card
PVA glue
Stickers
Gold glitter glue
White card blank

A simple design like this can be adapted to suit almost any party theme.

Football card

The decorations for this card can be made with rubber stamps or, if you don't have any available, can be drawn freehand. Use your child's favourite football team strip or adapt to any other game that is enjoyed in the family.

Making the card

1 Cut a piece of green card slightly smaller than the card blank and attach it.
2 Stamp two footballers and four footballs using black ink and leave to dry.
3 Cut out the footballs and attach to the corners of the card, using foam pads if you want a 3-D effect.
4 Colour the footballers with the crystal lacquer pens. Cut them out when dry.
5 Write or stamp the party message on narrow white card and mount it onto a larger piece of green card and then onto black card.
6 Stick the layered message card and the footballers onto the green background.

You will need
Green, white and black card
White card blank
PVA glue
Rubber stamp of footballer and football (or you could draw them yourself)
Blank ink pad
Foam pads (optional)
3-D crystal lacquer pens

Using cut-out pictures mounted on foam pads gives the card extra impact.

You will need

Red and pearlescent white card
Yellow card blank
PVA glue
Spotted white paper
Red ribbon
Brads

Colour card

This is a simple card that uses spotted paper and brads (coloured split pins) to make a colourfully dotted card. If you are having a themed party, keep an eye open for paper that features suitable pictures and motifs in place of the spotted paper.

Making the card

1 Cut a piece of red card slightly smaller than the card blank.
2 Cut spotted paper slightly smaller again and glue it to the red card.
3 Stick a piece of red ribbon across the middle of the paper.
4 Make small holes at either end of the glued ribbon using a hole punch or small scissors. Insert a brad through each hole and fasten.
5 Write or stamp a brief message on a piece of pearlescent card cut to the width of the ribbon and stick it to a slightly larger piece of red card.
6 Attach the layered message card to the ribbon and then glue the layered card to the card blank, tucking the ribbon ends beneath the red card.

Using spotted paper saves you lots of fiddly sticking and ensures a regular pattern.

Tropical card

A brightly coloured card has been made using layers and suitable stickers. With so many different designs of sticker being available from shops and more specialist outlets, it would be easy to adapt this design, should you want to.

Making the card

1 Cut a piece of green card slightly smaller than the card blank and attach it.
2 Apply a sheet of background paper slightly smaller again, so that the green card forms a frame.
3 Print your party message onto striped green card and mount it onto a larger piece of yellow card. Stick this onto the bottom of the card in the centre.
4 To make the beach scene, cut green card 10 x 12cm (4 x 4¾in) and glue this to the background paper, centred above the message. Then cut yellow card for the sand and blue card for the sky just smaller than the green card.
5 Apply the tropical stickers.

You will need
Green, yellow, blue and striped green card
White card blank
PVA glue
Background paper
Tropical stickers

You can create many different scenes using simple backgrounds and stickers.

You will need

Dark pearlescent pink, pale pearlescent pink and white card

Pale pearlescent pink gatefold card blank

PVA glue

Handbag and shoe rubber stamps

Pearlescent purple and pink ink pads

Shoes and bags card

This is a very 'girly' design, but use different colours and stamps and you've got a card that any young chap will happily flourish in the playground.

Making the card

1 Cut two strips of dark pearlescent pink card 4.5 x 20cm (1 3/4 x 8in) and stick them to the 'gates' of the gatefold blank, meeting at the central edge.

2 Randomly stamp shoes and bags in purple and pink onto white card. When dry, cut this to 8 x 19cm (3 1/4 x 7 1/2 in) before cutting it in half lengthways.

3 Stick these two 'gates' in place, making sure the pictures are complete where they meet.

4 Print the party message on white card 6.5 x 4.5cm (2 1/2 x 1 3/4 in), layering it onto first pale, then dark pink pearlescent card.

5 Glue this to one 'gate'.

A gatefold card has a sense of anticipation. What is written behind the doors?

Pink fairy card

This single-fold card has a layered, 3-D front and the edge is decorated with a rubber stamp. To tear mulberry paper, wet it with a paintbrush, then place a ruler on top to guide the rip.

Making the card

1 Cut a 3cm (1¼in) strip from the outside face of the card blank.

2 Using the fairy stamp and pearlescent pink ink, print fairies down the exposed inside edge of the card.

3 Cut a piece of white card 3 x 9cm (1¼ x 3½in) and write a short message such as 'Invitation' on it.

4 Glue it onto a slightly larger piece of pink card, and then another, larger piece of white card to create layers.

5 Tear a sheet of mulberry paper to make a piece even larger and then cut a final piece of white card slightly larger again.

6 Tear pink card to 9 x 16cm (3½ x 6¼in) and colour the edges with the ink from the ink pad. Leave to dry.

7 Stick together all the layers of card and mulberry paper and apply to the card blank.

8 Wrap six 90cm (36in) strands of yarn or ribbon around the centre crease, tying them in a bow in the top left corner.

You will need
Card blank
Fairy rubber stamp
Pearlescent pink ink pad
Pink and white card
PVA glue and gluestick (for the mulberry paper)
Pink mulberry paper
Ribbon and yarn selection

Torn edges and strands of yarn add texture and visual interest.

4 Decorations for your party

Decorating the party space makes it special, and this is where you'll be grateful you chose a party theme as it should inspire lots of ideas for what to do. There is plenty of advice here about how to bring a sense of celebration to the party room. This can be tiring work, however, so remember to book as many helpers as you can for the job well in advance and, as always, give the birthday child a role.

Decorating for a party

The whole point of a party is that it is a special day when everything is different, so it makes sense to make your house look as good as possible. Here we consider ways to decorate both the outside and the inside of your house.

Outside the house

▶ A 'happy birthday' banner will help people to find the right house and set the mood.

▶ Use big sheets of paper or paint an old sheet.

▶ Balloons tied to gates, fence posts and doors add a touch of jollity, too.

A piñata is ideally set up outdoors, where mess and noise don't matter.

▶ If you can put up some outside lights, so much the better. Even Christmas tree lights strung across a window makes the house seem different.

▶ Tie streamers to trees, gates, swings, sheds, cat flaps, dog houses – in fact, to whatever you can.

Piñatas

These are popular in America and increasingly popular elsewhere. A piñata is a papier-mâché and card model (often in the shape of a donkey or similar animal) decorated with coloured crêpe or tissue paper and filled with sweets, dried fruits and nuts or gifts. A traditional game is to hang the piñata from a tree and get blindfolded children to strike it with a stick until it bursts, showering the guests with treats. Since it is brightly decorated, it makes a lovely centrepiece for your decorations before being smashed to pieces.

Inside the house

Even if you are not playing games inside, children need space to roam, and excited children tend to roam at speed, so put the furniture around the edge of the room. If you are short of seats, cushions, pillows and rugs will be fine and will also help the room look special and different. Clear clutter, especially anything breakable, and any toys that would not be suited to the party, for example computer consoles, which are not appropriate for groups of children.

If you have pets, you may need to find somewhere for them to be out of the way. You may also want to make the room special by adding fragrances if there are some to go with your theme (a princess party could be scented, for example). Think about lighting, too: if you are having games that involve children performing (as in Charades, page 97), some kind of spotlight might be a nice extra touch. Have a designated area for coats and shoes.

Streamers

▶ Tie streamers so they loop along walls or from corners to a light fitting.
▶ Lay different colours back to back and twist them as you move to the next place where they will be attached.
▶ Crêpe paper makes wider streamers for that bold statement. Tie these quite taut: they absorb moisture and tend to droop after a while.
▶ Suspend lengths of crêpe paper or streamers from doorways so that they look like strings of beads.

Balloons

Balloons and parties go together like icing and cake. Tying up a few bunches of balloons is a quick, cheap way to make your house say 'Party!'
▶ Always hang balloons in bunches.
▶ Tie balloons to light fixtures (remove the bulb first for safety), doorways, door handles, chairs and anywhere else that can hold a knot.
▶ Decorate balloons with stickers or felt pens.

▶ Tie balloons with colourful ribbons and curl the ends.

▶ Tie a balloon to each child as he or she arrives!

▶ Use balloons to hide tape or glue used on other decorations such as streamers.

▶ Helium balloons that rise up (because helium is lighter than air) are really festive. However, some balloons lose their gas quite fast and start to deflate, so pick them up or have them delivered just before your party.

▶ You can buy animal- or other shaped balloons.

More decorations

Making your house look special for the party is part of the fun. Involve your child in choosing what to decorate with, perhaps giving her her own area to do. This will keep her interested while also building up the excitement about having a party. Choose colours to fit your theme – for example, blacks and orange for Halloween, bright yellows and greens for a tropical jungle. You might decide to really go to town and create a whole room set.

Home-made bunting

This is a good idea for making decorations to match your party theme and one that your child can get busy with in the days before the party. Cut or decorate pieces of card according to the theme, create a hole with a hole punch, then tie them about 30cm (12in) apart on a length of string or ribbon (or you can just staple them in place). Hang them like streamers. You could spell out a name or a message like 'Happy birthday!'

Costumes

Even if you haven't asked your guests to wear a costume, it is fun to have costumes for you, as host, and your child and other adults in your house, and sets a playful tone. After all, costumes are just decorations that you happen to be wearing.

▶ A hat, sunglasses and a colourful or themed T-shirt might be all you need.

▶ Paint faces to match the party theme.

▶ Wear party decorations in your hair.

▶ Stick on a temporary tattoo.

A few simple decorations can make a space look special and exciting.

Decorating the table

Eating the party food marks the centre point of the party. Children like food and know that their party spread is going to contain a lot of their particular favourites. They also love the novelty of seeing a table set just for them, with lots of fun decorations. So it really is worth making an effort to get the table looking inviting.

Have fun

Decorating the table is probably more important than decorating the other rooms, so if you are working to a tight budget, concentrate on this. Do talk to your child and try to think what she notices and likes on a table. If she generally appreciates novelty tableware, go for that. If she simply doesn't notice or care, save your money.

Protect the table

Children can be mucky eaters and excited children are pretty well bound to be especially messy, so make sure your table is protected from spills and stains. A plastic tablecloth should be sufficient but you might want to double it up with a vinyl one underneath. You should certainly do this if you are using a paper tablecloth. If you really want to keep mess and fuss to a minimum, give each child his food in a lunch or cake box. If your menu is all finger food, they won't need knives or forks either.

Seating plan

It may seem over-formal, but a seating plan can save a lot of problems. Everyone will want to sit next to the birthday child, and will be anxious to bag a place, so there could be an unseemly rush for seats. So prevent this from happen by having place settings instead.

Children love to see their names written out for them. You can do this in advance (it could be a job for your child), which also gives you the chance to ask your child who he would most like sitting nearest him.

▶ Give out party favours by placing these in named bags at each child's place, so they know where to sit and get a little present too.

▶ Take a Polaroid picture (or a digital one if there's someone who can then whisk the camera away and print the pictures) of guests as they arrive, and put one in each place at the table. It can then be re-cycled as a lovely memento for each child to take away when she leaves.

Decorating choices

Decide how you are going to serve the food ahead of sorting out the table decorations.

▶ If you are going to lay out all the food on the table for children to help themselves, there won't be room for many decorations and the food itself will make the table look bright and colourful.

▶ If you are going to serve the food in stages, or get children to help themselves from a separate table, buffet style, you will want to decorate the otherwise bare table. Pick one or two of the ideas that are given overleaf.

good to know

Party hats
Party hats are a traditional extra that children really enjoy. Again, many suppliers sell themed ones, or they are fairly easy to make by folding card into a cone shape, gluing it together, and tying ribbons or string through holes punched with a hole puncher.

A centrepiece focuses attention on the table.

A centrepiece

You might want to stick to one main decoration, a centrepiece in the middle of the table. This could be something relating to your party theme (a pirate or cowboy hat filled with goodies, for example) or even some of the birthday child's favourite toys (maybe some fashion dolls, or a teddy bear). If you have got a piñata (page 80), it could form your centrepiece.

Tableware

Parties are tiring for the host. You don't want to face a mountain of dishes to wash afterwards, so disposable tableware is a real boon. However, if you've got a dishwasher and know you'll be running a few parties over the next couple of years, invest in some bright plastic picnic ware and use that. You can buy brightly coloured or themed sets of plates, cups and bowls quite cheaply, and plastic knives, forks and spoons come in many colours. It is worth it. Children love drinking straws, too, and these come in bight colours, or novelty shapes if you prefer. It is probably worth just putting out plates and cups first and saving bowls for later as children can get carried away and fill every available container with food. In addition:

▶ Give each child their own table mat, perhaps just of decorated paper (another job for your busy child in the run-up to the party!).

▶ Lay curls of ribbons on each place setting.

▶ Have a spray of streamers or ribbons coming away from the centrepiece.

▶ Tie a balloon to every chair, or to the birthday child's chair.

▶ Children like fiddling with little novelties. If you have some, attach them to the tablecloth or chair with clothes pegs.

▶ Add a light sprinkling of confetti, which always looks festive.

Napkins and napkin rings

Napkins make any meal a bit of an occasion, and many party suppliers sell themed or coloured napkins for children's parties. Making a decorated ring to hold them is a thoughtful touch that some children might really appreciate.

▶ The simplest napkin ring is just a ribbon tied into a bow.

▶ A bagel makes a perfect napkin ring.

▶ Make napkin rings by cutting up the cardboard tube that paper towels are wrapped round. You – or you child – can decorate this by painting it or with stickers.

Party bags

Some parents find organizing the party bag more stressful than anything else to do with the party. Maybe this is to do with the expectation when children come to parties that they'll stagger out of that door laden down with a big bag of treats. Guests arrive with presents, so there is an element of giving something back.

Prize bags

If you don't want to go the party bag route, but feel you should give children something, how about a prize bag?

▶ If you are playing games during the party, you can give prizes.

▶ If you give prizes for 'best effort' or 'loudest cheer', you can make sure everyone gets something.

▶ You don't have to say what the prize is at the time (you could have been really organized and prepared named party bags in advance). Just tell the child, 'You've won a prize and it will be in your prize bag when you go home,' and they'll be happy and you'll know you've been fair to everyone.

It's the thought that counts

When planning the contents, an important factor is numbers. Party bags for eight or ten seems fair enough. But if you've ended up inviting the whole class from school plus a few outside friends and a cousin or two, you could break your budget on party bags alone. At the same time, look at the contents of a party bag from a child's point of view. They'll enjoy the party, but will also be that tiny bit happier if they go away with something – and nine times out of ten it doesn't matter too much what it is.

Party bags issued by venues that host parties tend to feature sugar, plastic and a not a lot else. You can buy better bags from specialist suppliers, or do the job yourself and still not break the bank. Do not include any items that could be a choking hazard for very young children.

Children can be anxious that they are going to miss out, so you could display named party bags near the door as people arrive, so that they all know they'll be getting something. They could even put any prizes of sweets they win during the party in the bag if they don't want to eat them there and then. You can also give out party decorations such as balloons and streamers as the children leave.

Presentation

Children love to unwrap presents, so even a modest party bag will be well received if it is in a smart box tied up with ribbon. Save gift bags or boxes at Christmas or from other birthdays. Writing the child's name on a tag shows you have thought of them, allows you to personalize your present if you wish, and ensures you don't miss anybody out (this is obviously a major sin).

One lovely idea is to make some simple bean bags covered in colourful fabrics. These can be used in any throwing games you play, and the children can be given one at the door to take home. It is better to give these out, rather than let children choose, as some children may be disappointed if they feel they didn't get to pick the one they wanted.

Attractive presentation shows someone has taken care to make you feel special.

What should go in a party bag?

Choose from these options:

▶ Something sweet to eat, like mini packs of chocolate buttons.

▶ Something that makes a noise, such as a whistle or a party blower.

▶ Something to play with, like a small toy.

▶ Something to read or write in, like a little notebook.

Prize biscuits

If you decide not to have party bags but want the children to have something to take away, how about getting them to decorate their own biscuits or small cakes, and then take them home? Make it the last part of the party for the children to come to the kitchen, choose their (really big) biscuit or small cake, and decorate it with a selection of sweets, cake decorations and icing (which works as glue).

▶ Something to write or draw with.

▶ Something to wear, such as a hair slide or bracelet.

▶ If you set a party theme, your party bag could reflect this. So if the theme was colours, include some coloured marbles or threading beads, and if your theme was animals, small model animals would be suitable.

▶ If you are really feeling generous, vouchers to see a film or buy a pizza would go down well with parents as well as children.

▶ If it is the holiday season, or your theme was tropical, make a cheap plastic bucket the party bag and add a spade for fun.

Supermarkets and discount shops often have toys and trinkets at low cost. Buy them when you see them – they are bound to come in handy, either as a party bag item or for your kids to enjoy on a wet day.

Giving them out

If they are to be handed out at the door, it is a nice gesture for the birthday child to do the giving. If the packaging or gift is delicate, a stock of plastic bags to pop them in might be useful. Having a lucky dip is a very old method of giving out gifts. Half fill a bucket or tub with sawdust, hay or shredded paper, and then pop in some wrapped presents, and the guests take one out as they leave.

For a more complicated way of distributing presents, write each guest's name on a piece of paper, place it inside a balloon which you then inflate. Release the balloons and tell the children to pop them one at a time. Whoever's name is on the paper gets the next present or turn at the lucky dip.

Any large container is fine for a lucky dip, but a see-through one allows a glimpse of the goodies lurking within.

5 Party games

Decide in advance what games you'll play, and the likely order. Plan for more games than you expect to play. That way you can adapt to suit the needs of the children, and you won't run out of activities. Obviously you'll need to sort out in advance any equipment needed, and have a clear idea of how each game is played. It might be better not to run through each game with your child ahead of the party, though, as this might be viewed by the other children as unfair coaching. Adapt the games to suit your party theme, by renaming them and the equipment (for example, target cones can become aliens for a space party, or treasure chests for a princess party).

Let's have some fun

Children love games. They come just a few notches down from the cake in the list of what a children's party must have. However, games need organizing, some of which can be done in advance, but they do put pressure on the party host to sort out teams, explain rules and ensure fairness.

Games checklist

▶ Is the game right for the guests' ages and abilities?

▶ Is it safe?

▶ Is there enough space?

▶ If the game is noisy, can it be played outside to save everyone's eardrums?

▶ Have you got the right equipment?

Ice-breakers

It is possible that not every guest will know the others, so start with some games where children have to exchange information or interact, so that they get a chance to meet everybody. If you start such a game as soon as a few guests have come, the party will get off to a calm, controlled start, and children can join in as they arrive. This is better than having everyone mill around waiting for something to happen.

Slow, slow, quick, quick, slow

Plan a mixture of calm and lively games, and switch between the types of games throughout the party. If you just opt for quiet circle games, some children will get frustrated at the restriction – they need to run about a bit. If you just have lively games of movement, there is a risk some kids could get wildly over-excited and become tricky to handle. So plan to have one or two calm games, followed by not more than two lively games. Varying the style of game in this way also gives more children a chance to shine, rather than repeatedly admiring the fastest mover.

Pace yourself

It can be hard work running (and playing) games, so you, as well as the children, may well need a break. Schedule games around other activities such as eating, opening presents, etc. Have games in different parts of the house or garden so that children stand up and move to the next location. This gives everyone a little break. Keep games short – even if one is a great success, don't be tempted to repeat it immediately, as children get bored very quickly. You could always play it again at the end.

Prizes

Some children are incredibly competitive and will want to win every game, and tell everyone how many they have won so far. This might be great for them, but not a lot of fun for other kids.

▶ Don't keep teams the same throughout the party – mix them up to help children to mix and to avoid over-competitiveness.

▶ Award prizes for things like best effort, biggest smile, careful listening and patience so that everyone has a chance to be rewarded.

▶ Pencils and toys are better prizes than sweets, which are likely to lead to hyperactivity as the winners experience a sugar rush.

▶ Don't keep a running score: it puts too much pressure on in this setting.

It's fun to do silly things!

Acting games

Most children love a chance to show off and get a bit of attention, so they adore acting games. They can get a bit carried away with this type of game, so keep it moving on – use phrases like, 'To make it fair', and, 'So everyone gets a go', as children appreciate the idea of fairness.

Act the tale

Ages: **6**+ Numbers: **9**+

▶ A lively game where children act out parts of a story.
Put the children into groups of three. Any extra children can double up with another member of their team. Each team must have a father, mother and child. As you tell the story (see below), each child must perform the actions of their character as they are mentioned. Pause after you mention each character, and make as many moves as you like. Change the child's name to whoever's party it is. The story reader judges which group did the best acting.

Variation: Tell any story you like, making sure you give the characters interesting actions to do.

Suggested story:

Dad was cooking sausages and sliced his finger by mistake. Mum was outside playing football and had just scored a great goal, so she didn't hear the terrible scream. (Name) was in his room painting the walls red, and he came rushing down the stairs, still holding the dripping paint brush. Dad looked up and jumped in fright. 'What have you done?' he cried. (Name) looked down. He was covered in paint and looked like a wounded soldier. Mum rushed in, tripped over the dog and trapped her head in the sink. (Name) tried to pull her out, but only managed to pour paint in her ears. Dad realized he still had all his fingers, but now the dog had taken the sausages, so he chased him round the room. In the end, Mum escaped from the sink. (Name) washed off most of the paint, and Dad finished cooking. But that sauce was very red and EVERYONE felt a bit ill afterwards.

Charades

Ages: **7+** Numbers: **5+**

▶ A famous traditional miming game. One person shows with gestures whether they are acting a film, television programme, a play or a book. Then she shows by holding up the appropriate number of fingers how many words are in the title and which word she will act, or whether she will act it as a whole. She can act part of the word by showing how many syllables it has (tapping an appropriate number of fingers on the opposite forearm) and which they are miming. It is worth getting someone to whisper the answer to the child at the start of each turn, to avoid any confusion later on. That person can also help with the gestures at the start. The audience has to guess the title being acted out.

Variation: Widen the choices to allow any word at all.

It's a film...

It's on television...

It's a book...

It's a play...

Cops and robbers

Ages: **7**+ Numbers: **8**+

▶ A quiet game using only the eyes.

One person is sent out of the room – he is the tracker. Write 'cop' or 'robber' on pieces of paper and give one slip to each player so that there is an equal number of cops and robbers, but they mustn't know which is which. Hide an object in the room and invite the tracker in. The robbers must sit still but steer the tracker towards the object with their eyes. The cops have to work out who the robbers are and accuse them. Whenever they guess correctly, that robber drops out of the game. The game ends when either the object is found, or all the robbers have been identified.

Frozen laugh

Ages: **3**+ Numbers: **6**+

▶ A lively game best played in a circle.

Throw a piece of fabric (such as a handkerchief) in the air. The children have to laugh constantly until it lands, when they have to freeze into silence. Anyone who makes a noise is out, until there is only one player left, or until it is clearly time to move on!

Variations: 1 Throw a feather or a toy on a parachute. **2** Stop and start silly music as the cue.

Living mirror

Ages: **4**+ Numbers: **6**+

▶ Less a game, more a drama activity that is good for children who can concentrate well, although you could award prizes for the best pair.

In pairs, children agree who will be the 'mirror' and who is the 'reflection'. The latter must copy every movement made by their partner. Feet must stay still at all times. Call out a series of actions, such as brushing your hair, tying a shoelace or eating spaghetti. Swap roles regularly.

Variation: Put on music for the 'mirrors' to move to.

Sleeping lions

Ages: **3+** Numbers: **10+**

▶ A quiet game good for calming down. Choose a judge, possibly an adult. All the children have to lie still as if asleep. If the judge sees you move, you're 'out'. The winner is the last child (or children) 'asleep'.

Who's in charge?

Ages: **6+** Numbers: **6+**

▶ A lively game with several variations. One child goes out. She will be the guesser. The others agree on a leader, whose movements and actions they start to copy. When the guesser returns, she has to pick out who is leading the group.

Living mirror is a calm game requiring concentration.

Variations: 1 The actions must all be silent. **2** The actions are rhythms, which can be created using any part of the body.

Zoo game

Ages: **3+** Numbers: **4+**

▶ A simple and quiet animal miming game.

Ask for a volunteer and whisper the name of an animal in their ear. They have to mime that creature silently and the children must guess what it is.

Balloon games

Balloons and parties go together like icing and cake, so it adds to the fun to use them in a game or two. Collect up scraps from burst balloons immediately as they are a choking hazard.

Balloon presents

Ages: **3+** Numbers: **Any**

▶ An unusual way to give out leaving presents.

Wrap one present for each guest and just write a number on the package. Write the numbers on small pieces of paper, and place one each in a balloon which you then inflate and seal. As the party ends, release the balloons and let each child burst one, revealing the paper slip. The child takes the present with the same number as the paper slip.

Quick feet win the day in the lively game of Bang!

Bang!

Ages: **5+** Numbers: **Any**

▶ A balloon-popping game for two players.

Tie a balloon to the left leg of each player. The aim of the game is to burst your opponent's balloon with your free leg.

Variations: 1 Try playing with more people. They could play individually or as a team (with balloons of the same colour for each team). **2** The balloons must be tied around the stomach.

Catch it

Ages: **6**+ Numbers: **6**+

▶ A balloon-catching game best played in a circle or with the players in a line.

Give everybody a number to remember. Drop a balloon and as you drop it say one of the numbers. That player tries to catch the balloon before it lands.

Variation: Say two numbers so there is competition to catch the balloon.

Catch me!

Ages: **5**+ Numbers: **Any**

▶ An ice-breaking activity.

Get each child to write his name on an inflated balloon (make sure each is legible). When you play some music, he throws up his balloon and tries to keep it or any other balloon up until the music stops. Then he catches the nearest balloon, reads the name and find its owner.

Hit the target

Ages: **4**+ Numbers: **4**+

▶ A simple balloon-launching game that can be played in teams.

Set up or agree on a target, which could be a picture or object related to your party theme. Give everybody an uninflated balloon and ask them to blow it up without tying the knot (younger children will need help with the inflating). On an agreed signal, everybody lets off their balloons, trying to fire them at the target. You can, if you wish, award marks for who gets nearest the target (with a bonus for hitting it).

Variation: Play in teams, with each team having balloons of the same colour.

---

must know

Blowing up balloons

Blowing up a lot of balloons can make you dizzy and give you a headache.

▶ Don't pull on the balloon first, as this can damage the latex and make it more likely to burst.

▶ Hold the balloon with your palm down, as this will protect your eyes if it bursts (or wear glasses). Use the other hand to gently ease the balloon away from you.

▶ Keep your cheeks flat and try to blow from your stomach, not from your head.

▶ The hardest part is starting off, so as soon as you have a bubble of air in there, stop blowing, hold the balloon tight to keep in the air while you rest, then try to inflate the balloon in one go. Even if you accidentally let out the air, the balloon will be easier to inflate second time around.

▶ Put off? You could always invest in a pump!

must know

Unequal teams
If you can't get teams of equal numbers, just select one player in the smaller team to do the action twice. If the teams are unequal in terms of skills, create a handicap for the stronger team, like having to hop.

Hockey

Ages: **6+** Numbers: **Even**

▶ A highly competitive balloon-hitting game.

Each player has a round balloon of a different colour, plus a long balloon which will be the bat or stick. Set up a goal – it can be an open box on its side. The aim is to 'score' by hitting the round balloon into the goal. You'll need to referee this one carefully.

Make a face

Ages: **4+** Numbers: **Any**

▶ A drawing activity using balloons.

Everybody has a balloon and a felt tip pen. Each child draws the hair on her balloon, passes it on and draws the eyes on the next one, and the nose on the next, and so on. You could tie each balloon to a chair at the dining table.

Variation: Play the game blindfolded.

Mine's bigger!

Ages: **5+** Numbers: **Any**

▶ A simple balloon-blowing activity.

Give everyone a balloon and ask them to blow it up as big as they dare. If one bursts, they're out. The biggest balloon wins.

---

watch out!

Balloon safety
Children choke more easily than adults, and balloons do represent a choking risk.
▶ Avoid using balloons at all with children under four years old.
▶ Store balloons – whether inflated or not – away from children.
▶ Pick up bits of burst balloon straight away.
▶ Polyester balloons (sold under the trade name Mylar) are safer than latex.
▶ Dispose of old balloons safely.

Musical balloons

Ages: **5**+ Numbers: **6**+

▶ A balloon version of Musical chairs (page 116).

Blow up enough balloons for all but one of the children. When the music starts, the children must pat the balloons in the air. When it stops, they catch a balloon, and one child will be 'out'. Continue until you have a winner.

On your head

Ages: **8**+ Numbers: **6**+

▶ A relay race with a difference.

Choose two or three teams of equal numbers. Agree a race course, which each team must walk along with a balloon balanced on their heads. If it drops, they have to let it land, then pick it up and replace it.

Variations: 1 Turn the course into an obstacle race. **2** The balloon must be held between the knees, or batted in the air.

Pass the balloon

Ages: **5**+ Numbers: **Any**

▶ A balloon version of Pass the parcel (page 110).

Players sit in a circle. While the music plays, they pass the balloon to each other behind their backs. When the music stops, whoever has a balloon in his hands is out of the game.

Passing a balloon behind your back is harder than it sounds!

Keeping a balloon in the air and following a race course is a skillful business.

Pass the sausage

Ages: 4+ Numbers: **Equal teams of 4+**

▶ A balloon-passing game.

Put the children in lines with a 2m (2yd) gap between each child and give the front players a long balloon each. The balloon must be kept between their knees, and they must walk to the next player in line and pass it on.

Patting race

Ages: 4+ Numbers: **Any**

▶ A simple balloon race.

Agree on the course and start the children off, each of them patting his balloon in the air. If it hits the ground, or if he hits another child's balloon, he has to start again.

Penalty!

Ages: 4+ Numbers: **Any**

▶ A balloon-kicking game that is best played indoors as wind will blow the balloons around.

Set up a goal. Place a balloon a short distance from it. Young children can just try to kick their balloon into the goal. Older children must be blindfolded. If they are very skilled, turn them round (blindfolded) a few times, at which point the game is great fun to watch!

Shot put

Ages: 5+ Numbers: **Any**

▶ A simple weighted balloon throwing game, to be
played outdoors.

Mark a circle on the ground. Fill balloons with
a little water (the same amount in each one), mark
them with each child's initials and ask children to
stand in the circle and throw their balloons from it.
The balloon that travels furthest wins.

Sunburst

Ages: 5+ Numbers: **Any**

▶ An outdoor balloon-bursting activity.

This only works if it is sunny. Tie up one balloon
for each child at a height she can easily reach (a
washing line is useful for this), and give each child a
magnifying glass. The child uses the magnifier to
concentrate the sun's rays until they burn through
the balloon and it bursts.

Volleyball

Ages: 7+ Numbers: **Equal teams**

▶ A highly competitive team game.

Set up a high net (a washing line will do) and
have two teams play volleyball over it with balloons.
Allow up to three or four hits of the balloon before
it is returned over the net. A point is scored if the
balloon hits the ground on the opposition's side. You
could mark out a playing area with cones if you wish.

Variation: Put children into pairs, each with a
towel. One side launches a balloon that is one-third
filled with water over the net for the other team to
catch in their towel and return. If the balloon bursts,
they lose.

must know

I don't like balloons
Some children dislike balloons,
hating the squeaky noises they
make when they are handled
and the bang when they pop.
You could invite such children to
be judges, or to work with a
partner, or have some distracting
activity such as a bottle of soap
bubbles.

Circle games

Children are used to sitting in a circle for various activities at school, so some circle games might make nervous children feel more secure. It is also a good chance for you to learn names and get familiar with the children at the party. So a circle game or two is a good way to kick off.

Beat my name

Ages: **3+** Numbers: **Any**

▶ A good ice-breaking activity for children who don't know each other.

Each child says her name, and the rest of the group claps back the rhythm of the name, e.g. Jack has one beat, Seejal has two, Stephanie has three. Offer help to shy participants.

Blind man's buff

Ages: **6+** Numbers: **8+**

▶ A very old identity-guessing game.

Blind man's buff has been a party favourite since its introduction as a Victorian parlour game.

You need an obstacle-free area to play this. Blindfold one child and put him in the middle of the circle. Everyone in the circle keeps moving round in one direction until the 'blind man' claps three times, points at someone and guesses her name. If he is correct, they swap places. If not, the child comes into the circle and the 'blind man' has to catch her and guess her identity by feeling her face, hair and clothes.

Variations: 1 Players circulate singing a song. The 'blind man' claps, points at someone and tells her to do something such as, 'Cry like a baby' or 'Say the alphabet', after which he tries to guess the performer's identity.

Categories

Ages: **7+** Numbers: **6+**

▶ A quick-thinking word game.

A player chooses a category such as 'song titles', 'sports' or 'colours', then calls out a word that fits the category. Each player in turn has to find a suitable but different word until someone fails and a new category is selected by that player. Decide from the start whether players can be 'out' or not.

Variations: 1 As well as finding words, players have to clap and snap their fingers in a set rhythm. **2** Allow players to roll (not throw!) a ball across the circle to determine who has to find the next word.

Coat game

Ages: **4+** Numbers: **10+**

▶ A fun observation game.

Children sit in one large group, not a circle. One child leaves, and you cover up a volunteer with a

must know

Making a circle
▶ Many children are used to getting into a circle through school activities, but if it is all a bit slow and hesitant, get everyone to line up behind you and tell them to follow. Walk in a circle shape and say 'Stop!' They should now be standing in a rough circle which you can adjust as necessary.
▶ If best friends sitting next to each other get distracted, ask everyone to sit next to someone they don't know very well to make new friends That will calm things down.

large coat. The child returns and guesses who is under the coat.
Make it trickier by moving everybody around when the guesser has
left the room.

Crash!
Ages: **3+** Numbers: **Any**
► A simple game for young children that is fun for all to watch.
  Blindfold one child and give her a wooden spoon. Put a saucepan
(or a cymbal or any other object that makes a noise when hit)
somewhere near her. She bashes around with the spoon until
making a crash.

Duck, duck, goose
Ages: **3+** Numbers: **6+**
► A lively traditional chasing game.
  Choose a 'fox', who walks around the outside of the circle,
tapping each child on the head and naming them 'duck', until he
changes this for one child to 'goose'. The goose must chase the fox
around the circle and tag him before the fox completes the circuit
and sits in the goose's place. If the fox is tagged, he repeats his role.
If not, the goose is the new fox.

Eat the choc
Ages: **4+** Numbers: **6+**
► A very lively chocolate-eating game.
  In the middle of the circle, place a big bar of chocolate on a plate,
a knife and fork, hat, gloves and scarf. Children take it in turns to roll
the die and if someone gets a six she has to put all the clothes on
and eat the chocolate with the knife and fork. While she is doing this
the others continue to roll the die and anyone throwing a six takes
their place.
  Variations: 1 For large groups, use two dice and double the
number of clothes. **2** Use chocolate buttons with younger children.
3 Use oven mitts instead of the other clothing.

The tension builds up in a game of Eat the choc. Will she get a delicious mouthful before someone else throws a six?

Hot potato

Ages: **3+** Numbers: **6+**

▶ A passing game for young children.

Children pass any object around the circle. It can be a ball, beanbag or even a potato. They have to imagine it's hot and so must pass it on quickly. When an adult helper calls 'Hot!', whoever is holding the 'potato' is out, and play continues.

Variations: 1 Use music to signal when to start and stop. **2** Play outdoors with a water-filled balloon (change of clothing required!).

Name bash

Ages: **3+** Numbers: **Any**

▶ A good ice-breaking game.

One player stands in the middle of the circle (the seeker), holding a rolled-up newspaper. An adult calls out the name of one child, and the one in the middle has to find that child and bash him with the paper. But if the child named calls out someone else's name before being reached, the seeker has to find her instead. When someone has been bashed, she becomes the new seeker.

As a test of flexibility Packet pickup is a good game when it is time to calm down a little.

Packet pickup

Ages: **6+** Numbers: **Any**

▶ A test of flexibility.

Put an empty cereal box in the middle of the circle, open side up. Each child in turn has to pick up the box with his teeth, without touching it or the floor with his hands or knees. After each round, tear a strip from the top of the box, making the stretch required longer. See if the children can get right down to the bottom strip.

Pass the parcel

Ages: **3+** Numbers: **Any**

▶ A lively traditional game.

Prepare a parcel with a present loosely wrapped in many layers of paper (newspaper is fine). Allow at least one layer per person. Play some music while the children pass the parcel round. Whenever you stop the music, the child holding the parcel removes a layer of wrapping, until the present is revealed.

Variations: 1 Place a small gift in each layer, so more people get a prize. **2** Write forfeits (see box on page 138) on slips of paper and put one between each layer. **3** Tell children to close their eyes while the parcel is being passed. Then they have the fun of seeing who has it when the music stops. **4** The parcel must be passed behind their backs. **5** Turn the game into 'Eat the parcel' by putting a sweet between each layer. You could even use edible rice paper for some of the layers! **6** Use bags inside each other and call it 'Pass the bag'.

Ring round the ring

Ages: **3+** Numbers: **6+**

▶ An old treasure-hiding game.

Take a long piece of string or fishing line, thread a ring or bead onto it and tie it to make a large circle, which the children sit around, holding the string in their hands. One child leaves the room and when she re-enters she stands outside the circle while the children pass the ring along the string secretly. You call 'Stop' and the child guesses who has the ring.

Ticket man

Ages: **6+** Numbers: **8+**

▶ A lively seat-swapping game that needs some preparation.

Have a set of place names (they could be on postcards or just pieces of paper) and a sheet with a list of them. Give all but one of the players a postcard. Everyone sits in a chair in the circle apart from the 'ticket man' who stands in the middle, holding the list. He calls out two places, and the players holding them have to swap seats before the ticket man can sit in one of the empty seats. Whoever is left standing is the next ticket man.

Variation: Use animal pictures instead of place names.

Who swapped?

Ages: **4+** Numbers: **8+**

▶ A quiet memory game.

Blindfold one child and sit her in the centre of the circle. Give all the others a piece of paper with a number or letter on it. Call out two numbers or letters, and those two children must swap places, passing the child in the centre. Then she removes her blindfold and guesses who swapped.

Zoo queue

See Speaking and listening games, page 136.

See Speaking and listening games, page 136.

---

must know

Fair play

In any game where music is played and stopped to give children a go, it is vital that you play fair, and are seen to play fair. You could turn your back and leave things to chance, but children will think it very unjust if someone gets two goes while others miss out. One way round this is to 'manage' the music so that a new child gets a turn each time, until the final round, when you turn round and let fate take its course.

Drawing games

Many children really enjoy drawing but might not expect to do it at a party, so playing some drawing games will be a lovely surprise. Drawing games also tend to be quite calm, which can be a relief during a busy, excited party.

Blind drawing

Ages: **4+** Numbers: **Any**

▶ A simple, funny drawing game.

Blindfold half the guests. Give them pencil and paper and tell them what they are going to try to draw – choose something that relates to your party theme. You could just give them a minute to draw it, or instruct them what part they should put in next, asking them to remove their hand between each bit of sketching. The other guests can enjoy watching the drawings appear, then it's their turn.

Watching what someone draws when she is blindfolded can be very funny indeed.

Draw round me

Ages: 3+ Numbers: 9+

▶ A good ice-breaking activity.

Put the children into teams of three or four. Give each team a large piece of paper (lining wallpaper is perfect) and felt tip pens. Send each team to a different part of the house and ask them to draw around one person and colour in the features and clothes. On their return, other teams guess which child was the model.

Drawing consequences

Ages: 6+ Numbers: **Any**

▶ A game that results in funny drawings.

Ahead of the party, fold sheets of A4 paper widthways in half and half again so that the creases create strips going across. Open out the paper. Sit the children in a circle and tell them they are going to draw something to do with your party theme (e.g. an alien, an animal or person). Give each of them two felt tips and a sheet of paper. Tell them to draw the head first, drawing the lines of the neck going over the top crease. Then they fold what they have drawn back out of view and pass the sheet on. The next player draws the shoulders and arms using the neck lines as a guide, folds and passes. Next comes the body (tops of legs going below the next crease), and then the legs. Now they can open up the pictures and see what they look like.

Variation: Fold the paper so that it has five creases, making six strips to draw on.

New planet

Ages: 3+ Numbers: **Any**

▶ A quick drawing game.

Give everyone an inflated balloon and a felt tip pen. Tell them the balloon is a new planet, and they have to populate it with aliens. Award prizes for the most aliens and the most careful drawings.

must know

I can't draw
Some children, like some adults, are convinced they can't draw and may be reluctant to take part in these games. Reassure them that the game is not a test of ability, and that the aim is to have fun. Point out that quite often good artists are not very good at drawing games as they try to perfect their picture, rather than knock it out fast.

Pass the drawing

Ages: **6+** Numbers: **Any**

▶ A drawing version of the popular game of Chinese whispers (see page 136).

The first player draws something (it can be anything) on a piece of paper and shows it to the next player for ten seconds. That person then has to draw what he saw, show it to the next player, and so on. The fun is in comparing the first with the final drawing. Make sure only the next person sees the picture. You could play this game during the meal, calling over the next player one at a time.

Songdraw

Ages: **6+** Numbers: **Teams of 4-5**

▶ A drawing version of Charades (page 97).

Prepare in advance cards on which you write the titles of songs (such as carols at a Christmas party) that everyone is likely to have heard of. Put the children into teams and give them a pencil and paper. One person from each team comes to you to look at the card (you can whisper the title if necessary), then returns to draw the title for her team to guess by singing the song.

Superfast drawing

Ages: **8+** Numbers: **Teams of 3 or more**

▶ A lively, fast drawing game.

This is a version of the popular board game 'Pictionary'. Before the party, prepare some cards with words or phrases, perhaps related to your party theme. For example, if it is a pirate party, have cards for 'plank', 'skull', 'flag', 'treasure' and so on. You need at least 20 cards. Divide the group into teams, each with a pencil and paper. One person from each team comes to you and you show him a card. He must return to his team and draw it so that his team-mates can guess the word. No gestures

or speaking are allowed. Award points for correct answers if you wish, but this game need not be competitive.

Tell me what to draw

Ages: **6+** Numbers: **Any**

▶ A pairs game.

Put the children into pairs sitting back to back, one blindfolded and with a pencil, paper and something to rest them on. Give the other child an object. She has to describe it, while her partner tries to draw what he hears. Swap roles. You'll need quite a few objects so that none are used twice.

What's my dot?

Ages: **3+** Numbers: **Any**

▶ A simple drawing activity for all ages.

Give each child paper, felt tip pens and a stick-on dot. Everybody sticks the dot somewhere on their piece of paper and completes a drawing using it. Each child can then show his picture and explain it.

Musical games

The introduction of sounds adds an extra dimension to games. Most (but not all) children love singing and listening to music, and are much les self-conscious about performing than adults.

Musical chairs has long been a party favourite.

Find your partner
Ages: **6+** Numbers: **10+**
▶ A lively racing game.

Put the children into pairs, and then organize them so there is an inner circle of children facing their partners, who are in an outer circle. When the music starts, each circle must go round in the opposite direction to the other (agree this first!).

When it stops, children race to pair up with their partners.

Musical chairs
Ages: **3+** Numbers: **6+**
▶ A traditional, lively racing game.

Make a line of chairs, each slightly apart and facing the opposite direction to its neighbour. Each child stands by a chair. When you play the music, children must march in the same direction around the chairs. While it plays, remove one chair. When you stop the music, everybody sits down in the nearest chair, leaving one child 'out'. Continue until two players race to sit in the one remaining chair.

Variations: 1 Have two rows of

back-to-back chairs, or chairs in a circle. **2** Put
the chairs into two separate circles and tell the
children they must walk in a figure of eight around
these. **3** Pillows, cushions or large sheets of paper
can be used instead of chairs. **4** Use items of
clothing or hats, that children must put on instead
of sitting down.

Musical statues

Ages: **3**+ Numbers: **6**+

▶ An old 'catch you out' game.

Tell the children they have to move about and
dance to the music, but must freeze into a statue
pose as soon as it stops. Anyone who moves when
there is no music is 'out', and could help you judge
the next round.

Variations: 1 When the music stops, it is a race
to sit on the floor. **2** When the music stops,
everybody has to stand on one foot, or have one
hand on the floor.

Name that tune

Ages: **6**+ Numbers: **6**+

▶ A song-recognition game that requires advance
preparation.

Collect songs that most of the children will have
heard, so material from the charts and a few nursery
rhymes if you have them. You could record them
onto tape or burn a disc with them, but otherwise
just collect them as CDs or in another format and
make sure there is no packaging that would identify
them. Children can work in teams or on their own.
Play a short burst from the start of the song and
invite guesses as to what it is. Keep doing this until it

is identified. You could give extra marks for speed or for naming the artist, or stating the year it was made.

Variations: 1 Write out some lyrics and read them for children to guess. **2** Choose older songs that have the title as part of the lyrics. **3** Tape songs and jingles from TV and radio stations.

Pass the parcel
See Circle games, page 110

Singalong
Ages: **3**+ Numbers: **6**+

▶ Singing songs on their own is fun, but check out the ideas for variations too.

Young children in particular love to sing, and you could just enjoy singing old favourites such as 'Wheels on the bus', 'If you're happy ...' and 'Old Macdonald'.

Variations: 1 Prepare a big picture of a traffic light showing the colours red, orange and green. When you point at green, everyone sings the song. When you point at orange, everybody claps the rhythm of the words. Red means the song carries on in your head, and when you change colour everyone tries to pick up with where the song should be. **2** Give groups of children 15 minutes to come up with new words to the tune of a well-known song, then perform it.

Spot the leader
Ages: **6**+ Numbers: **8**+

▶ A fun rhythm and observation game.

One child leaves the room to become the guesser. Put on some music and choose one child to lead the others clapping along, but he must change the rhythm regularly, and which body part he hits. When the guesser is invited in, she tries to work out who is leading the clapping.

Variations: 1 Put children in a circle to make it harder to spot the leader. **2** Instead of clapping, have a dance leader.

Talent show

Ages: **6**+ Numbers: **6**+

▶ A chance to perform for those who wish to.

State on the party invitation that children can prepare a short song or part of song to perform, and run this as a talent show. Clap every performer and find a way of giving everyone a prize (such as for 'hardest words to learn', 'biggest bow to audience').

The tambourine game challenges musical and listening skills.

Tambourine game

Ages: **5**+ Numbers: **6**+

▶ A rhythm-tapping game.

Demonstrate how you can tap the rhythm of a name, giving one hit per beat or syllable (so Fireman Sam is two hits followed by one hit). Children tap the rhythm of someone else's full name and everybody has to guess who it is. Get them to whisper it to you first so you can help with the rhythm and ensure everyone will know the name.

Variation: Tap the names of pop stars or other famous people (you might drop in a clue or two).

Outdoor games

Playing games outdoors allows children to let off steam and gives your ears a rest from the excited noise of an indoor party. A garden is ideal or use a local park, provided it is a safe environment. Have one helper per five children for outdoor activities.

Choosing teams and pairs

Having captains to choose teams means there will be children left feeling like rejects, which won't exactly make your party a fun place for them. Guests at a children's party don't all necessarily know each other, so asking them to pair up isn't easy either. Keep the event happy and smooth-running by following these tips:

▶ When you need pairs, choose them yourself, deliberately pairing up children who don't know each other well. If you let them pick their best friend, some will feel left out, and the competitive stakes will be higher.

▶ One trick for finding pairs or teams is to say, 'I need a volunteer.' All the hands shoot up, and you start choosing from there on.

▶ If you need, say, three teams, give each child a letter: A, B or C (red, blue, green teams). Then all the As go together, as do the Bs and Cs. You can also do this with colours, foods or use your party theme. The point is that it is fair and random.

▶ If you need equal numbers in teams and have an odd number of guests, double two children up, or invite one to referee. If it is a relay, one child in a smaller team can have two goes.

▶ Remember, letting children choose teams, even if it is their birthday, is divisive.

Baby race

Ages: **6**+ Numbers: **4**+

▶ A very silly racing game.

　　Set out two chairs each with a bib and a bowl of mushed-up food (fruit purée is popular) with a plastic spoon. Divide the children into two teams and sit them down 10m (10 yd) from the chairs. When you say, 'Go!', the

first two children in each team run to a chair, one puts on the bib and the other feeds her. First back to their team with the bib removed wins. If you have plenty of bowls and purée, you could set this up as a relay race.

Children find it hilarious when someone has to pretend to be the baby.

Broom game

Ages: **6+** Numbers: **Any**

▶ A dizzy activity that is very funny to watch.

Ask someone to stand in the middle of an open space and give him a broom. He must hold the brush high, bristles in the air, and turn around it ten times, looking up at the bristles. Then ask him to walk to you across the space. He will find this very difficult! Grass is the best surface as people tend to fall over.

Bucket goal

Ages: **4+** Numbers: **Any**

▶ A simple throwing game requiring lots of balls.

Set out a row of buckets. There could be one for each child or team, or you could use coloured buckets and have a scoring system. Children have to stand behind a line and throw balls into the buckets. Make it fair by having them line up and go to the back of the queue after each throw, successful or not. The softer types of low-bouncing ball are better because they won't rebound out of the bucket.

French cricket

Ages: **5**+ Numbers: **4**+

▶ A simple racket and ball game.

You can't move your feet in French cricket.

Give one child a tennis racket. She is the batter and must stand with her feet together without moving them at all. The rest of the children are bowlers and fielders. One of them throws the ball, aiming at any part of the batter's foot or leg below the knee. If the ball touches any of these areas, or if the batter moves her feet, she is 'out'. Likewise, if the batter hits the ball and it is subsequently caught, she is 'out', otherwise whoever picks up the ball must bowl from where it landed.

Variations: 1 If fielders catch the ball after one bounce, the batter is out. **2** Allow younger children to move their feet to turn to face the bowler.

Grandmother's footsteps

Ages: **5**+ Numbers: **Any**

▶ A traditional and calm game of movement.

One child goes to the end of the space and stands or sits with his back to the others, who line up at the other end. They have to creep up and tap the child ('grandmother') on the shoulder, but he can turn round at any time and say the names of anybody he saw moving. They must return to the start point. The person who taps grandmother on the shoulder becomes the next 'grandmother'.

Variation: Put out two or three coats and divide the children into that number of teams. Whoever touches the child must be wearing the coat. If they work as a team, they can hide each other as someone puts it on.

How much did you spill?

Ages: **5+** Numbers: **Any**

▶ A water-carrying game, with variations (see photograph on page 11).

Mark two lines of five circles with chalk or use hoops or cardboard to make five stepping stones just too far apart to step across easily. Children have to move along the stepping stones carrying a full plastic cup of water. The winner is whoever has the most water left. You could also play as a relay race.

Variations: 1 Children have to wear flippers.
2 They also have to carry a book on their head.
3 They get on all fours and pass through hula hoops with a plastic bowl of water placed on their backs.

Kick bowling

Ages: **4+** Numbers: **Any**

▶ A mixture of soccer and bowling skills.

Set up five skittles (or large plastic bottles half filled with water) in a 'V' formation. Children have to

good to know

Play my game
Sometimes children want to play their own games. This is obviously fine provided everyone understands the rules – which is often not the case with a group of children from different places. Get the children to explain the rules to you and their fellow guests, as this will prevent confusion and remind everyone of how to play. If you don't want it to go on forever and there is no obvious conclusion, set a time limit (oven and microwave buzzers are good for this – get a child to set one).

kick a ball from a set distance and see how many skittles they knock over. This can be played individually or in teams. Adjust according to ability by having different types of ball (e.g. soccer or tennis ball).

Skateboard race

Ages: 4+ Numbers: **Any**
▶ A race using this popular toy.

The basic version of this game is to set out a course and get the children to race it on skateboards. However, if you then set terms such as, 'You must sit on the board at all times' or 'A partner must push you along', you can make up variations that allow even non-skateboarders to take part.

Water and spoon race

Ages: 5+ Numbers: **Any**
▶ A water transporting race.

Place two bowls filled with water at one end of the space and two empty plastic glasses at the other. Members of each team take turns to race to fill the glass, transporting the water with a spoon.

Variations: 1 Colour the water with food dye to fit a party theme.

Water bowling

Ages: 5+ Numbers: **Any**
▶ A simple water-throwing game.

You need a start line with a bucket of water 5m (5yd) away, and some skittles (plastic bottles with a little water for stability will do) about 3m (3yd) further on. Children take it in turns to run to the bucket, fill a plastic cup from the bucket and throw the water to knock over the skittles.

Wear the lot race

Ages: **4+** Numbers: **6+**

▶ A relay race with a difference.

Put the players into two equal teams and give each one a suitcase or bag filled with the same amount of all types of clothes – in large sizes, the stranger the better, but all items the children can put on and take off themselves. On your signal, the first player in each team puts on all the clothes, runs with the empty suitcase to an agreed place at least 10m (10yd) away, removes the clothing and returns it to the case, then runs back to their team. Each player takes a turn.

What's the time, Mr Wolf?

Ages: **5+** Numbers: **Any**

▶ A traditional chasing game for young children.

One person is Mr Wolf, who stands at one end of the space. The others call out, 'What's the time, Mr Wolf?' and he says a time between one and 12 o'clock. The children have to take that number of steps. However, when the wolf replies 'Dinner time!', he chases them and whoever he catches is the new wolf.

The more bizarre the combination of clothes, the better for the Wear the lot race.

Races

Children love the thrill of competition, and provided you don't make too much of a fuss of the winners and encourage taking part, they should all enjoy these games. This section comprises different kinds of races that do not involve running. Some of these can, of course, be played outside, too.

must know

Team mixing
Try not to keep teams the same throughout the party. The atmosphere will become very competitive and some children will find it daunting. Instead, mix up team games with individual and paired activities, and when the time comes for a new team game, select fresh teams.

Ankle race

Ages: **5+** Numbers: **Any**

▶ A surprisingly tricky race!

Set a course to race, and the only condition is that children must hold their ankles throughout. This is great fun to watch.

Blow it

Ages: **3+** Numbers: **Any**

▶ A game that needs lots of puff.

In advance, prepare some paper shapes about the size of a postcard that match your party theme. Put one in front of each child, and his job is to blow it over an agreed finishing line.

Variation: Children send the shape as far as they can with three puffs.

Chopstick race

Ages: **5+** Numbers: **Any**

▶ A test of manual dexterity.

Give each child ten sweets, a bowl and a pair of chopsticks. She must get the sweets into the bowl using the chopsticks.

Variation: Hold the chopsticks in one hand.

Double packers

Ages: **7+** Numbers: **Pairs**

▶ A tricky present-wrapping game.

Each child must hold the hand of the other in the pair. Give each of them an object such as a shoe box or book, a sheet of wrapping paper or newspaper, sticky tape and a ribbon. They must wrap up the 'present' using their free hands. First pair wins.

Dress me up!
Ages: **4+** Numbers: **Any**
▶ A team dressing-up game.

Put the children into teams, each with a set of clothing. The aim of the game is for them to dress one child in their team in as many items of clothing as possible in two minutes. Those being dressed are not allowed to do anything themselves.

Flap the kipper
Ages: **3+** Numbers: **Any**
▶ A very old paper-flapping game.

Cut large kipper shapes in newspaper, and find somewhere with a hard floor. Put one kipper in front of each child, who should also have a folded newspaper. He cannot touch the fish, but can flap his newspaper to make it 'swim' across to the finishing line.

Flap the kipper can be adapted to party themes by changing the shape of the paper object being raced across the room.

Hot or cold?

Ages: **4+** Numbers: **Any**

▶ A traditional treasure-hunting game with clues.

Hide a sweet in the room, which the children must search for. You provide a running commentary of who is 'hot' (close) and who is 'cold' (way off), until the prize is found. Repeat.

The Knee-jerk relay can be played with almost any unbreakable object between the knees – try balloons or ping pong balls.

Jacket race

Ages: **6+** Numbers: **Any**

▶ A dressing-up race.

Place two chairs back to back. Hang a jacket with the sleeves turned out on each, and lay a rope along the floor underneath them. A pair of children have to run up to the chairs, put the jacket on and do up the buttons, then cross to the other side and pull out the rope to end the game. If both grab the rope at the same time, the game is a draw.

Variation: Substitute clothes that tie in with your theme, like a pirate's outfit.

Knee-jerk relay

Ages: **6+** Numbers: **6+**

▶ A very silly racing game.

Put the children into equal teams. Give the first player in each team an object, such as a ball or an orange. She must complete an agreed course with the object held between her knees, returning for the next player to do the same.

Variation: If one team is more skilful at the race, give them a smaller object like a matchbox or marble to carry.

Obstacle course

Ages: **4+** Numbers: **Any**

▶ A long-loved furniture-climbing activity.

Remove anything breakable! Set out a course involving traveling round the room, going over and under the furniture. Children can either go round it on their own, perhaps being timed to find the fastest, or as a paired race.

Variations: 1 Children travel the obstacle course blindfolded. You could give them a helper offering instructions and a helping hand where necessary. **2** This is more of a stunt, and you can only do it once. Set up the course, show it to two children who are then blindfolded. While they prepare themselves or are distracted by someone perhaps offering 'helpful' guidance, move the furniture to the middle of the room, or even take some out. Watching them attempt the course in thin air is hilarious.

Orange race

Ages: **7+** Numbers: **Any**

▶ A very silly fruit-moving race.

Two children each need a leg of an old pair of tights and two oranges. One fruit is placed down one leg of the tights, which are then tied around the waist. Swinging this as a 'bat', children then race to tap their other orange across a finishing line.

Variation: Try this with a broom pushing a ball.

Paperclip race

Ages: **7+** Numbers: **Any**

▶ A chain-building race.

Give each player a set of paperclips and show them how to link them to make a chain. How long a chain can they make in one minute?

Variations: 1 How quickly can you make a chain of 30cm (12in)? **2** Do this as a team relay game with children adding a paperclip then passing the chain on.

good to know

Pacing races
Races are exciting and children can get a little over-wrought with them, so plan the games to have a lively race, followed by a quieter, calmer game, and so on.

Ping pong relay

Ages: 5+ Numbers: **Equal teams**

▶ A fun race using table tennis balls.

Put the children into teams, half of each at either end of the room. Using a straw, the children must each blow a ping pong ball across the room to their team-mate, who then blows it back. Children must travel on all fours as they follow their ball.

Variation: Try using a slightly larger but light ball.

Shoes and coats race

Ages: 5+ Numbers: **Any**

▶ A perfect game to finish the party.

Pile up everybody's coats and shoes in one mountain, making sure to separate pairs of shoes. The race is to find your own clothes and put them on before anybody else. Children will cooperate more if you play this in teams.

Snap!

Ages: 4+ Numbers: **Any**

▶ A hide-and-seek card game.

Hide the cards from a whole deck around the room. Deal a second pack out to the children, making sure they each get an equal number of cards (so you may need to keep a few back). The race is for them to find each matching card to make a pair. They can call 'Snap!' every time they find one, and the game is over when someone has a complete set.

Variations: 1 Use fewer cards for young children **2** Use a 'Happy Families' or similar family card-game pack.

Stepping stones

Ages: 8+ Numbers: **Equal teams made up of paired children**

▶ A stepping-stone relay race.

Ahead of the party, cut a big pair of feet out of card for each team and work out the course for the race. Divide the teams into pairs, and each of these must decide who is the 'footman' and who the 'stepper'. Give each team a pair of feet. The footman places the feet in front of the stepper, who must only walk on the card pieces as she goes around the course. When they return, the next pair goes.

String race

Ages: 5+ Numbers: **Any**

▶ A simple hide-and-seek game.

Hide different lengths of string around the room. The children have to find them and tie them together. The winner is the one with the longest length. Young children may need help with the tying.

Suck the peas

Ages: 3+ Numbers: **Any**

▶ A pea-moving race.

Each child has a straw plus two cups, one full of peas. The aim of the game is to suck the peas onto the straw and drop them into the other cup.

Stepping stones calls for cooperation within the pair.

Treasure hunt

Ages: 3+ Numbers: **Any**

▶ A traditional hunting game that requires preparation.

In advance, hide various items around the room (or several rooms would be more fun). Prepare a sheet showing what you have hidden, in writing or pictures. Children race to find as many items as they can. You can tie in the objects with your party theme. Make it clear which parts of the house are included in the game.

Variations: Award points for each item, but give bonuses for finding them in bright colours, or small sizes, etc.

Running games

Some children really need to run around to let off steam, and running games allow them to do this in a controlled way without getting too wild. These games are best played outside or indoors in a suitably large, obstacle-free area.

watch out!

Safety and running games
Don't let children play running games in bare feet or, worse, in socks. They can slip and hurt themselves very easily. Carpets are also not ideal surfaces for games where children can fall, as they can skid and get a painful carpet burn.

Below the knee

Ages: **7+** Numbers: **Any**

▶ A throwing and running game probably best played outdoors.

One child has a soft ball. They throw it, aiming to hit other children on or below the knee. Anyone hit joins them and they work as a team until everyone has been hit.

Variation: No moving when you have the ball.

Bowl race

Ages: **4+** Numbers: **Equal teams**

▶ A relay race with a difference.

Put the children into equal teams and have a bowl of buttons or beads (or objects that match your party theme) for each team. Set the bowls at one end of the running area, and put all the teams at the other end with an empty bowl for each. One child from each team runs and collects a button, putting it in the empty bowl. This is the signal for the next child to go, and so on, until the first bowl is empty.

Variations: 1 Use sweets instead of buttons. **2** Add a handicap like having to hop, or run backwards.

Chain race

Ages: **5+** Numbers: **Equal teams**

▶ The whole team ends up running together in this lively race.

Set two cones or chairs a good distance apart. Divide the children into equal teams and put one behind each cone. The

first child in each team runs a circuit round the opposite cone and returns to his team. No one is allowed to obstruct him. For the second circuit, hi must run holding hands with his next team-mate. This is repeated until by the final round the whole team is running, all holding hands.

The Chain race can be adapted for many party themes – it could be called Caterpillar race, or Train race, for example.

Dressing-up relay

Ages: **6+** Numbers: **Equal teams**

▶ A fun variation on the standard relay.

Put a set of outsize clothes out for each team. If it matches your party theme, so much the better. The first child in each team puts everything on, runs the course and removes the clothing for the next child to take over.

Duck, duck, goose

See Circle games, page 108.

Fox and chickens

Ages: **6**+ Numbers: **Any**

▶ This much-loved chasing game needs a lot of space.

Choose the first 'chicken' and a 'fox'. The chicken goes to the far side of the space, and calls out the name of any child. She is the next chicken and must try to get across without being caught by the fox. Captured chickens have to stand still.

Go for the string

Ages: **6**+ Numbers: **Any**

▶ A race to get the prize.

Place two chairs about 3m (3yd) apart and facing away from each other. Tie a prize like a bag of sweets or a toy in the middle of a long piece of string and lay this string so that it runs from under one chair to the other. Players sit in their chairs, then, on a signal, race round their opponent's chair, sit down again and the first person to pull the string gets the prize. Show the children the direction they should run in so that they can't collide.

Obstacle course and skills race

Ages: **6**+ Numbers: **Any**

▶ Adapt this sport's day classic to your party theme.

With a bit of imagination you can make a pretty good obstacle course and tie it in with your party theme. Children can crawl under old sheets (peg them loosely to the ground), jump over canes resting on buckets, etc. Put in a skills section too, like balancing a ball on a bat, or bouncing a rugby ball.

Tag

Ages: **5**+ Numbers: **Any**

▶ A very old game of catch.

One child is 'it', and must catch the others by touching them, when they become fellow catchers until there is one child left. That child starts the next game.

Variations: 1 Children who are tagged must 'freeze' and can be released by other children tapping them, or squeezing through their legs. Anyone tagged three times becomes a catcher. 2 Tag by jumping on someone's shadow (this needs a sunny day and a watchful referee!).

Three-ball relay

Ages: **6+** Numbers: **Equal teams**

▶ A relay race with a difference.

Give each team three balls – they can be different sizes. On your signal, the first child in each team travels the course, rolling the three balls as he goes. They can only touch the balls with his hands. He passes the three balls on to the next player, and so on.

Variations: Balls must be bounced or kicked.

Stay alert for the the Three-ball relay!

Wacky races

Ages: **4+** Numbers: **Any**

▶ Silly ideas for racing.

This can be played individually or as a relay. You just have to think of silly (but safe) ways for the children to run, such as with their hands on their heads, or sidestepping, balancing a toy on their head, in pairs with one leg tied together, backwards, while singing a song, and get them to do it. Have a few ideas ready and then ask the children: they'll have lots!

Speaking games

Speaking and listening games help children to develop social skills and are particularly useful at the start of a party as they make people talk to each other, break the ice and help everyone have a nicer time as a group.

Chinese whispers

Ages: **6**+ Numbers: **10**+

▶ A traditional speaking and listening game.

Prepare a few messages of at least ten words in advance. They can be silly or sensible. Children sit in a circle or a line and you give one child a message card (make sure she can read it). That child then whispers it to the next person, and the message is sent round the group. You could play music in the background to prevent anyone overhearing it. The last person says the message out loud and it is compared with the original.

Variation: Let children make up their own messages.

Chinese whispers is played in various guises all round the world.

Four elements

Ages: **8+** Numbers: **Any**

▶ A quick-fire throwing, thinking and speaking game.

Children sit in a circle with a leader in the middle, who has a ball. The leader throws the ball to another child, saying either 'Earth', 'Water', 'Air' or 'Fire'. The child has to return the ball while saying an animal (Earth), fish (Water) or bird (Air), depending on which element the leader said. If the word was 'Fire', he has to run around pretending to put out the fire. Punish mistakes with forfeits (see box on page 138), and change the leader regularly.

Happy birthday, your majesty

Ages: **4+** Numbers: **Large groups**

▶ A game where children guess who is disguising their voice.

Choose someone to be king (or queen), and stand him facing away from the group, or just blindfold him. Point to a child for him to say, 'Happy birthday, your majesty' in a disguised voice. The 'king' has to guess who spoke. Keep a tally and allow a few goes.

No, yes

Ages: **7+** Numbers: **Any**

▶ A game that requires quick thinking.

One child comes to the front and the others ask her direct questions such as, 'Do you like sausages?' or 'Can I have your sweets?' She can answer however she wants but she is not allowed to say 'Yes' or 'No', and she must answer within five seconds. Allow up to ten questions per child.

must know

Helping shy talkers

Some children can be very shy about speaking in front of others, particularly to groups of people. Here are a few tips to help them:

▶ To talk with them, move them away from the prying eyes of the group and get down to their level (but not too close as to be scary).

▶ Don't apply pressure on them to speak to a group; it will make things worse.

▶ Find the person the child feels most comfortable with (it may be another child or an adult) and ask if that person can speak out loud for the child.

▶ Let them sit in on speaking games but make it clear they don't have to talk.

▶ Try to give them choices, like, 'You can say your word to me or write it down on this paper' so that they don't feel as if they are on the spot.

▶ Set up a paired activity game (perhaps from the Drawing games, see pages 112–15) to help the child gain confidence.

good to know

Forfeits
Many of these games give you the chance to set forfeits if children get something wrong. Here are some ideas:
▶ Sing a song.
▶ Do a dance.
▶ Say the alphabet.
▶ Say the alphabet backwards.
▶ Do an impression of someone famous or someone you all know.
▶ Run around the outside of the house.
▶ Hop for 30 seconds.

Simon says

Ages: **3**+ Numbers: **Any**

▶ A very old copying game.

One person is the leader. He says, 'Simon says …' and adds an action, such as ' … put your hands on your head.' Everybody has to copy, unless the leader gives an instruction without starting with 'Simon says …', in which case no one should do it. Children are 'out' if they disobey these rules.

Smelly sausages

Ages: **5**+ Numbers: **Any**

▶ A game where children try to keep a straight face.

One child comes to the front. Children ask her questions and she must always answer 'Smelly sausages,' however little sense it makes. The child answering is 'out' if she laughs. Allow up to ten questions per child.

Variation: Change the phrase to something linked to your party theme, or insist the questions are to do with the party theme.

Straight face

Ages: **6**+ Numbers: **4**+

▶ The aim of this game is to keep a straight face.

Children sit or stand in a circle. One says 'Hee!' to his neighbour, who then turns to his neighbour and says 'Hee, hee!' Everybody has to keep a straight face while a 'Hee!' is added each time. Anyone who smiles or laughs is 'out', and can then go anywhere and pull faces at the other players, but not make any sounds. Eventually you will have a straight-faced winner.

Variations: 1 Allow the 'out' players to make noises too. **2** Change 'Hee!' to other phrases, perhaps related to your party theme.

Keeping a straight face can be quite an effort sometimes!

Twenty-second list

Ages: **8+** Numbers: **Any**

▶ A game for quick-witted fast talkers.

Have some ideas for categories ready in advance, such as 'colours' or 'sports'. They could tie in with your party theme. Ask children to name as many things as they can in that category in 20 seconds. Keep a tally so you can have a winner if you wish.

What animal am I?

Ages: **7+** Numbers: **Any**

▶ An identity-guessing game.

One person leaves the room and the others decide on a creature that they have to guess. When the child comes back in, she asks questions like, 'Can I swim?' and 'Do I have a nest?' The rest of the group can only answer 'Yes' or 'No.' The child has to guess what animal she is.

Variations: 1 Play this game as an ice-breaker at the start of

Following instructions when you're wearing a blindfold means you have to trust the speaker.

the party by sticking pictures or labels of animals on the children's backs. They have to ask the other children questions, and again, the answers must be 'Yes' or 'No.' **2** Instead of animals, you could choose objects linked with your party theme.

What's my line?

Ages: **8+** Numbers: **Any**

▶ A variation on a famous TV quiz show from the past.

One child goes out of the room, and the others choose an occupation that she will have to guess, for example teacher.

When she returns, she asks everyone in the group for something she must buy to do her job, and tries to guess the occupation from their answers. If she can't, in the next round she asks what she would wear. The game ends when she identifies the job. You need to make sure everyone understands what the job is before the questioning part of the game.

What's my product?

Ages: **8+** Numbers: **Any**

▶ A good ice-breaking game requiring some preparation.

Cut out advertisements for products children like, such as chocolate bars, toys. When each child arrives, stick or pin one advertisement to his back. He has to ask the other children questions about it to guess what it is. They can only answer, 'Yes' or 'No.'

Variation: Use the wrappers themselves.

Where am I going?

Ages: **7+** Numbers: **Equal teams**

▶ A lively race with instructions being shouted by a partner.

Divide the children into equal teams and set up a fairly small circuit. Remove any dangerous obstructions. One child in each team is blindfolded and the rest of the team call out instructions to send him round the course, when the next player puts on the blindfold and sets off.

Zoo queue

Ages: **4+** Numbers: **Any**

▶ A memory game that works best in groups of 6–10.

Children sit in a circle. The first says, 'One cat' (it doesn't matter what the animal is), the next adds to this by saying, 'One cat, two rabbits.' The game continues with children reciting all the numbers of animals, adding to the list each time. If they forget one, they are 'out', and the game continues.

6 Party food

Feeding other people's children can be worrying. What will they like? How much will you need? What if they won't eat a morsel? Then you've got the pressure of it being a party. How can the food match the theme? What about the all-important cake? Remind yourself that this is just part of the whole event, and that even if a child eats nothing, she'll probably have a great time. This section gives you plenty of ideas for party food to prepare as much as possible in advance and how to choose or make that all-important cake.

Managing the menu

The day of the birthday party is going to be pretty busy, so it is worth sorting out as much as possible of the food in advance.

must know

Essential party fare
▶ Sausage rolls
▶ Cocktail sausages
▶ Sandwiches
▶ Snacks
▶ Small cakes
▶ Jelly
▶ Drinks

Be kind to yourself

Here are a few general pointers:

▶ Although it is part of the event, the food is unlikely to be the main highlight for the children, so don't put too much pressure on yourself to produce a memorable Harry Potter-style feast.

▶ Children can be picky eaters so keep most of it simple – even if your child loves spicy dishes, you could end up with a lot left on the plates if her friends don't share her taste.

▶ There is an increasing number of children with food allergies (or awareness of them), especially of nuts, and nut allergy can kill. Check ahead if anyone has a food allergy, and if you're not sure, don't serve anything with nuts in it – and check labels carefully, as it can be surprising what foods do contain them.

▶ If it's a themed party, you can have fun making some of the food link with the theme, but don't go mad: pick one or maybe two themed items (say, shaped sandwiches and a special drink), and the rest can be normal party fare, which is less work for you.

▶ Use small plates – children tend to pile them with food and leave half of it.

▶ Get an adult to help you serve food, maybe taking care of drinks.

▶ The cake is the most important item on the menu, as that's where most attention will be focused. If you're not confident about cooking it, you can always buy slabs of cake to build your own creation, or of course you can buy in a ready-made cake (see page 164).

▶ If you go for hot food, cook it ahead and re-heat it on the day.

Empty plates

Excited children don't necessarily feel hungry, so there's no need to prepare loads of food, and it makes sense to use packets of shop-bought ones as much as possible to avoid waste as it won't matter if they're not eaten on the day. So, for example, use individual packs of pepperoni rather than sausages, packets of crisps rather than bowls piled high with them, and bought chocolate rolls rather than making a batch of cakes. However, there is also plenty of evidence that additives and food colouring affect children's behaviour, and they'll be fairly excited as it is, so simple home cooking has a lot going for it.

Sharing food teaches children many social skills … and it's fun!

Well done, everyone!

Children love getting rewards, so you could have stickers to give out to those who clear their plates or tidy up, even some jokey certificates for 'Best jelly eater', 'Cleanest spare ribs fan' or 'Emptiest plate'. Just make sure everybody gets some kind of reward, or there could be tears over the birthday cake.

DIY food

If no one else can help, you can always set up a 'make your own sandwich' system with bowls of ingredients and piles of sliced bread. The kids will probably find it fun – but it will be messy!

Sandwiches

Kids love sandwiches, especially when they look that touch different. You can make them a bit special or match your party theme through the fillings you choose, the shapes, or type of sandwich. Go for variety.

---

good to know

Sandwich fillings
You can play safe and use simple fillings if you know there are some picky eaters coming, but here are a few ideas for more unusual fillings:
- ► Tuna salad with sliced apple and raisins
- ► Chicken and redcurrant
- ► Green pepper and celery
- ► Ricotta cheese with orange segments
- ► Cheese and pesto or grated carrot
- ► Hummus with roasted red peppers or chopped olives
- ► Feta cheese with mint and cucumber
- ► Sardines with ketchup
- ► Cream cheese and sultanas
- ► Cottage cheese and chopped dates
- ► Banana and honey
- ► Banana and chocolate spread or honey

Your choices

Choose from a range of white and brown breads, small rolls or pieces of baguette, bagels, pitta bread, chapattis, tortilla wraps. Try two or three different types of bread in the one sandwich for a rainbow effect – mixing, say, white, multigrain, brown and rye, raisin.

Shapes for sandwiches

Shaped sandwiches really appeal to kids, and they look great piled up on the table. Use a cutter if you have one, or take your time with a sharp knife to cut, for example, bears, cars, fish, hands (put your hand into the bread and cut round the outline you made) or trains.

Open-topped

These give you the chance to have some fun making the topping fit the party theme, or just look different. For example, you could make a face using pepperoni slices for eyes and half a slice of stoned olive for the mouth.

Double deckers

Create a real party mouthful by making layered sandwiches: alternate layers of brown and white bread with perhaps more than one type of filling in between. Listen to the silent appreciation!

Pinwheels

These look really special and are excellent for themes that include circles, like sports or trains. Cut off the crusts and spread a thin layer of filling on each slice. Then roll it up tightly and put a toothpick through each one to hold it in place while it chills in the fridge. Just before serving, remove from the fridge and cut into small rounds.

Pinwheels are a pleasing variation on sandwiches.

Flatbread roll-ups

Basically the same as a pinwheel sandwich, this variation uses pitta bread instead. Take a piece of pitta and cut around the edges to separate it into two layers. Use each piece separately, placing fillings on the inside surface and make as for the pinwheel sandwiches.

Rolls and baguettes

You can match rolls to your theme or just make them look different by attaching food such as blueberries and olives with toothpicks to make eyes and a nose. Cut a slot in the bread and use it to hold watercress for hair. For more ideas, see the individual themes on pages 26–65.

Wraps

Use tortilla wraps or chapattis to create a wrap or rolled sandwich.

good to know

Wheat allergy/intolerance
Some children can't eat wheat due to allergy or food intolerance. Check in advance and ask them to bring an alternative.

Pastry and bread

Pastry can be cut to any shape and most kids love it, making it ideal for children's party food. Of course, you can make your own pastry, but buying it ready made (short crust or puff varieties) saves a lot of work and perhaps gives you more time for making a selection of different shapes.

Cheesy shapes

Preheat the oven to 200°C/400°F/Gas mark 6. Roll out the pastry and cut out your shapes. Brush with beaten egg and sprinkle with grated cheese. Bake on a greased baking sheet for 10–15 minutes until golden.

Cheese straws

Preheat the oven to 190°C/375°F/Gas mark 5. Either make pastry as you normally would or buy in ready-made puff pastry. Roll it out and sprinkle with grated cheese (orange-coloured cheese looks best) on one half. Fold over and roll out again. Repeat this. Then cut into strips about 1cm (½in) wide, which can be cooked as they are or twisted. Cook on an ungreased baking sheet for 12–15 minutes until golden. You can also curl the cut strips into spirals to make a pinwheel shape.

Filo pastry

Filo pastry is good for creating shapes, especially triangles like somosas, or 'bags of gold' where you pop a filling in the middle of a square of pastry then fold up the sides and twist them together. Filo pastry is very thin and is prepared by putting it into layers with melted butter painted between each one. This is a fiddly and it is well worth doing a 'dry run' and cooking a test batch before the party. Your family will be delighted to test it out!

Always put some of the driest ingredient in the bottom of the parcel, to stop the pastry getting soggy, then add the mixture on top. Possible fillings include:

▶ Minced beef
▶ Tomato and mozzarella
▶ Ricotta and spinach
▶ Mixed vegetables
▶ Nuts in syrup
▶ Walnuts in honey
▶ Pecans, syrup and orange rind.

Sugared bread fingers

Mix together 1¹⁄₂ tsp easy blend dried yeast, 500g (1lb 2oz) plain flour, ¹⁄₂ tsp salt and 1 tsp sugar and mix in 300ml (¹⁄₂ pint) warm water until a soft dough. Knead and shape into long bread sticks about 25cm (10in) long. Leave to rise covered with oiled cling film for 30 minutes and then bake at 200°C/400°F/Gas mark 6 for 6–8 minutes until golden. Drizzle with white or coloured glacé icing (page 158) and sprinkle with hundreds and thousands.

Sugared bread fingers can be coloured to match a party theme.

Meat dishes

Some kids are big-time carnivores and will expect to eat their
daily meat ration at your party.

Burgers and hot dogs

Bake a pile of burgers and sausages and let children put their own
burgers/hot dogs together using sliced baps and a range of relishes.

Chicken nuggets

First prepare the coating. Beat 2 eggs with 2 tbsp milk and mix with
100g (3½oz) breadcrumbs or flour. Cut 4 boneless skinned chicken
breasts into chunks or strips and dip them in the coating. Heat 2
tbsp cooking oil in a frying pan and cook the nuggets until browned.

Chicken drumsticks

These can be served with dips (page 156) or as they are, ready to eat
with the fingers. You can use thighs instead of drumsticks. All
recipes are for eight drumsticks. Be particularly careful to check that
the juices are clear and the meat no longer pink before serving.

**Chicken and ribs
will satisfy ardent
meat-eaters at
your party.**

Saucy drumsticks: For pleasingly garish drumsticks, marinade the scored drumsticks in a sauce of 2 tbsp each of ketchup and brown sauce, 1 tsp each of soy sauce and honey. Grill for 15 minutes, turning regularly.

Orange drumsticks: Fry the drumsticks in butter until slightly brown. Add 1 tbsp lemon juice, 2 tbsp orange marmalade, 150ml (¼ pint) orange juice, 3 finely sliced carrots, 1 tbsp cornflour, 3 tbsp brown sugar, seasoning and a little ground ginger if you wish. Mix together and leave to simmer for 30 minutes, or transfer to an oven and bake at 200°C/400°F/ Gas mark 6 for 30 minutes.

Sticky drumsticks: Marinade the chicken in 3 tbsp sunflower oil, 2 tbsp each of honey and soy sauce, and 1 tsp of mustard. Grill or bake as before.

Sticky ribs

Marinate 500g (1lb 2oz) pork ribs in 3 tbsp tomato ketchup, 2 tbsp soft brown sugar, 1 tbsp each of sunflower oil, Worcestershire sauce and mustard for 2 hours. Preheat the oven to 200°C/400°F/Gas mark 6. Put the marinated ribs in a roasting tin with 450ml (¾ pint) chicken stock and cook for an hour, basting occasionally.

Spicy ribs

Preheat the oven to 150°C/300°F/Gas mark 2 and bake 500g (1lb 2oz) spare ribs for an hour. Meanwhile, mix 2 squeezed cloves of garlic with 1 tsp shredded fresh ginger and 2 tbsp each of soy sauce and tomato purée, with 1 tbsp each of soft brown sugar and sunflower oil. Pour this sauce over the cooked ribs and return to the oven for about 30 minutes at 180°C/350°F/Gas mark 4 until crisp.

Lamb kebabs

Cut up pieces of lamb into chunks and skewer them along with a selection of vegetables. Grill or bake in a hot oven for 10–15 minutes, turning regularly. Don't serve on the skewers as these can be a hazard, but the children will enjoy these bite-sized morsels.

Pizza

Pizza is one of the most popular foods for children, so it guarantees smiley faces around the table. It is also quite easy to decorate pizza so that it looks a bit special or matches your chosen party theme.

Making the most of a pizza

▶ Buy ready-made pizzas (just simple tomato and cheese varieties) and add ingredients for decoration (see left).

▶ Frozen pizzas are easier for decorating as you can move them around without them getting floppy and ending up on the floor.

▶ Small pizzas are easier to serve as you don't need to cut them up.

▶ You can buy ready-made pizza bases.

▶ Use split toasted muffins, bagels or pitta bread as alternative pizza bases.

▶ Buy pizza mix (or use a dough recipe of your own) and make your own bases. This allows you to make smaller, individual pizzas if you wish, or to play around with the shapes and make, say, a square pizza, or one that displays the age of the birthday child or a house-shaped pizza. You can even wind the dough into a long sausage and make a snake-shaped pizza.

▶ Children may find eating pizza easier if you cut it up into bite-sized squares or triangles for them.

Decorating pizza

Spread the bases with watered-down tomato purée or a home-cooked tomato sauce and let the children

put the toppings on themselves. Just put a selection of ingredients in bowls and get them to do the rest – it could be something each child is invited to do as he arrives. Get the children to watch you putting the pizzas in to bake, and remind them to be sure which one is theirs! If decorating pizza yourself, go for big, simple shapes, because the toppings will melt or shrivel a little when they cook.

Plenty of children like salad or some of its ingredients, and it goes very well with pizza. Set up a salad bar, with lettuce, shredded carrots, grated cheese and anything else that might be popular. Put dressings into small pots or bowls – children can easily get over-enthusiastic if they are pouring or squeezing it from a bottle

Decorating their own pizzas is a great way to keep children busy and involved while the food is being prepared.

Potato and vegetable dishes

These provide nutritious and filling fare, which could be a good move if the party involves a trip out somewhere.

Branded baked potatoes

This really shows you've made an effort, and actually it is very easy. Preheat the oven to 200°C/400°F/Gas mark 6. Cut the initials of each child, or any symbol that matches your theme, into the skin of each potato before baking them with the cut side uppermost for 50 minutes. Small children will only need a half potato each.

Stuffed potatoes

Bake enough potatoes for everybody, then scoop out the flesh into a bowl. Mix with a little butter and milk and 50g (2oz) grated cheese per person. Return the mixture to the potato shells and cook for a further 10 minutes to brown. The finished stuffed potatoes can be decorated with vegetables and cheese slices according to your party theme. For example, you could add a face or other shapes – see the suggestions on pizza decorating on pages 152–3.

Shaped mash

Preheat the oven to 180°C/350°F/Gas mark 4. Shape mashed potatoes to match your theme (like a circle for 'sports', or a train) and place on an oiled baking sheet. Brush with melted butter, and bake for 10 minutes until browned. As a variation, add a beaten egg and grated cheese, fluff the mixture up, shape it and bake for 30 minutes. This produces a higher, bigger dish.

Herbie roasties

Preheat the oven to 190°C/375°F/Gas mark 5. Cut potatoes into small chunks and place on a roasting tray. Sprinkle with sunflower oil and dried herbs and bake for 45 minutes, stirring occasionally.

Potato shapes

These are a fine alternative to chips and excellent for dipping (see page 156). Preheat the oven to 220°C/ 425°F/Gas mark 7. Choose large potatoes, peeled and cut into thick slices. Use either a knife or shaped cutters to make any shape you like: stars, moons, numbers, dinosaurs. Place them in an oiled baking tray and bake for 30 minutes until browned, turning once.

Roasted vegetables

These are good hot or cold and make good dippers (see also pages 156–7).
Preheat the oven to 180°C/350°F/Gas mark 4. Cut vegetables such as courgettes, peppers, onions and aubergines into large chunks, drizzle with a little olive oil and bake for 30 minutes.

Potatoes can be cut into almost any shape, but you need to buy big ones to produce large shapes.

Vegetable fingers

Cut thick slices of courgette, pepper or aubergine and dunk them in flour, then a beaten egg mixture, then finally a bowl of breadcrumbs. Fry them in olive oil until they start to brown.

Stuffed peppers

This recipe calls for more preparation, but it looks great and is a good alternative if one of your guests doesn't eat meat. Preheat the oven to 180°C/350°F/Gas mark 4. Cut the pepper in half, wash and deseed. Fry finely chopped onion, mushrooms and any other vegetables of your choosing until they are soft. Mix them with grated cheese and place the mixture in the pepper halves. Bake for 20 minutes. These can be decorated as for Stuffed potatoes (see left). See also vegetable dipper recipes on page 156.

Dips

Children really enjoy dunking away at dips. They are also a great way to get kids to eat healthy raw vegetables, but in all honesty that's not really your priority at a children's party – it's a bonus. However, they are easy to make and serve and you can have lots of fun making dips to match your theme by colour, decoration or choice of ingredients.

Dip ideas

Avocado with cream cheese: Equal quantities of avocado, cream cheese, yogurt or mayonnaise.

Cheese: 200g (7oz) cream cheese, 150g (5oz) grated Cheddar, 2 spring onions (finely chopped), 1/2 tsp salt.

Creamy onion: 150ml (1/4 pint) sour cream, 2 spring onions (chopped), 2 tbsp soy sauce.

Cucumber: 1/2 cucumber (peeled), 1 tbsp fresh mint, 300g (11oz) thick plain yogurt. Add cumin for a curry flavour.

Hummus or taramasalta: Fine on their own.

Salsa: Finely chop and mix together 4 tomatoes, 2 spring onions, 1 green chilli with seeds removed, 1 clove of garlic (peeled), 1 tsp sugar, 2 tsp chopped fresh coriander or basil.

Smoked mackerel with cream cheese and lemon: 110g (4oz) cream cheese per fish fillet, add lemon juice and seasoning to taste.

Tomato: Ketchup with yogurt and chopped onion.

Tuna: 175g (6oz) tinned tuna, 110g (4oz) cream cheese, juice of 1/2 lemon, salt and pepper.

Vegetable: Chop and then blend 1 red pepper, 1/2 cucumber, 1/2 celery stick and handful basil with 300ml (1/2 pint) sour cream and lemon juice.

Perfect dippers

- ▶ Shaped crisps
- ▶ Corn chips
- ▶ Tortillas
- ▶ Breadsticks
- ▶ Strips of carrot, cucumber, red pepper, celery.

Fruit dips

Halve a melon and scoop out the seeds. Fill the
cavities with sweetened natural or fruit yogurt. For
dippers you could use any of these, perhaps held
with a toothpick:

- ▶ Sliced strawberries and bananas
- ▶ Raspberries, grapes or any other bite-sized fruit
- ▶ Mandarin orange segments
- ▶ Dried apricots
- ▶ Ice cream wafers
- ▶ Small squares of cake.

Fruit dips are tasty and healthy.

Small cakes and biscuits

Shaped or decorated cakes or biscuits can be the highlight of your party fare. You don't have to bake your own: shop-bought versions will be fine and you can still customize them to your party theme in the kitchen.

Queen cakes

This basic small cake recipe can be adapted and decorated in many ways. Preheat the oven to 180°C/350°F/Gas mark 4. Put 110g (4oz) granulated sugar, 110g (4oz) softened butter and 2 eggs into a bowl and then sift in 110g (4oz) self-raising flour and 2 tsp baking powder. Beat together for 2–3 minutes with a wooden spoon. If it is too stiff, add a little milk. Spoon the mixture into 12–15 paper cases and cook for 15 minutes or until golden brown. Allow to cool before decorating. For variations, see the biscuits recipe opposite.

The butterfly cakes on page 29 show just one way of decorating these small cakes to make them unique to your party. But you don't have to turn queen cakes into butterflies, you can just keep their tops flat, cover with glacé icing and then decorate. Using squeezy tubes of coloured icing is probably the easiest way of doing this, adding colour with sprinkle shapes.

Butter icing

This adds flavour and makes the cakes look really special. Sieve 225g (8oz) icing sugar into a bowl, add 110g (4oz) butter and mix with a wooden spoon until soft and creamy. Add food dye or fruit juice to create coloured icing to match your theme.

Glacé icing

This is an excellent icing for small cakes and biscuits and can easily be coloured and decorated – see page 167.

Biscuits are just right for face decorating. Faces are pleasingly easy to do. Use icing, sweets, glacé cherries, hundreds and thousands or anything else to make a face to match your theme.

Biscuits

Shaped and decorated biscuits are a good alternative to small cakes – people, teddy and animal shapes go down especially well. Preheat the oven to 180°C/350°F/Gas mark 4. Mix together 225g (8oz) plain flour with 110g (4oz) butter. Stir in 110g (4oz) caster sugar and 1 tsp vanilla essence. Then add a beaten egg and stir the mixture. Roll out the resulting dough, cut it into the shapes you want, and bake on a greased baking sheet for 12–15 minutes. Decorate when cool. Some extra ingredients could be:

▶ $1/2$ tsp ginger or cinnamon for a spicier biccy

▶ 25g (1oz) chocolate chips

▶ 25g (1oz) currants or raisins

▶ 25g (1oz) glacé cherries

▶ 1 tsp lemon juice and grated zest of half a lemon.

Jelly

Jelly and ice cream is one of the great traditional combinations for birthday parties. The wobbly stuff is facing more competition these days, but the different colours available and its capacity for holding interesting shapes and fruit or sweets still makes it a popular choice for birthday fare.

Things to put in jelly

▶ Using sweets like wine gums and shaped goodies that match the theme of the party work very well. The trick is to make about half the jelly and pour it into a clear glass bowl. When it is nearly set, push sweets in so they are held about half way down. Leave to set before adding the remainder of the jelly mix to set. Now the sweets look as if they are floating.

Given a bit of time, traditional party fare such as jelly takes on a new look.

► Fruit is great in jelly, too – use canned fruits but steer clear of kiwis and fresh pineapple as the jelly won't set.

► Add food dye to change the colour of the jelly.

► Put different fruits in each layer for a truly fruity and interesting jelly.

► Mix jelly with fromage frais for a creamier, opaque dessert a bit like fruit fool. As the jelly starts to cool, mix in 225g (8oz) fromage frais per 135g packet of jelly (see the photograph on page 42).

Things to do with jelly

► Shaped jelly moulds allow you to make individual, shaped jellies to match your theme.

► You could make your own mould using heavy-duty metal foil, supported in a mixing bowl.

► One time-consuming but spectacular trick is to pour a small amount of jelly into glasses, leave to set, then add other colours one layer at a time. A variation here is to tilt the glasses so that the jelly sets in diagonal lines.

► Fill half a glass bowl with half-set yellow jelly. Top up with half-set red jelly, cover with cling film and then shake to create a sunrise or sunset scene.

► Make frothy-top jelly. Put four cubes of jelly in a blender and add 225ml (8fl oz) boiling water. Cover and blend at a low speed for about 30 seconds until the jelly has dissolved. Add a handful of ice cubes and 225ml (8fl oz) water and stir until the ice is partially melted. Then cover and blend at high speed for about 30 seconds. Pour into individual dishes or a serving bowl and chill for 10–20 minutes.

► Add flavour by replacing the water with fruit juice, syrup from canned fruit, or carbonated soft drinks.

Fruit

Plenty of (though not all) children enjoy fruit and you'll certainly make their parents happy if you can get them to eat something reasonably healthy at your party.

Frosted fruits

Fruits such as plums and grapes look out of this world if you brush them with reconstituted dried egg white and dip them in caster sugar, creating a frosted effect. These are great for girly parties and ghostly themes.

Chocolate fruit

Melt some chocolate and dip half of fruits such as strawberries, cherries, seedless grapes and mandarin segments in the sauce.

These chocolate fruits look so good you could pop some in a party bag as a leaving treat.

Chill in the fridge, then serve in paper cases or just piled in a bowl. The result looks great, tastes fantastic and as long as they hold the uncoated side, the children's fingers won't get covered in sticky chocolate. This works for nuts as well, but such are the worries about children with nut allergies, it's probably worth playing safe and sticking with fruit.

Fresh fruit kebabs

Fruit looks really different if you chop it into chunks about 2.5cm (1in) across and thread it onto a plastic straw.

Dead man's fingers

Baking a banana in its skins turns the flesh deliciously creamy and the skin goes black – great for themed parties where you want something ghoulish. Serve with sugar and cream.

Fruit pizza

This is an unusual but tasty idea. Preheat the oven to 180°C/350°F/Gas mark 4. Cream together 110g (4oz) butter and 175g (6oz) sugar. Mix in an egg and stir in 175g (6oz) plain flour and 1 tsp bicarbonate of soda until you have a smooth dough. Press into an ungreased pizza pan, bake for 8–10 minutes until golden and then allow to cool. Beat 225g (8oz) cream cheese with 110g (4oz) sugar and 2 tsp vanilla extract, and spread this on the pizza base, finishing with any fruit you choose.

Fruit comes in all sorts of shapes and you can always cut it to make a shape that doesn't occur naturally. For ideas for fruit shapes to use for decorating your fruit pizza – or anything else – see right. Attach decorations with glacé icing (see page 167), cream cheese, or use a toothpick. To prevent cut fruit from turning brown, drizzle lemon juice on the exposed surface.

Fruit dips

See page 157.

good to know

Sweet shapes
► A pear halved lengthways makes a good body shape to which you can add arms and legs.
► Slices of star fruit make unusual-shaped heads or twinkling stars.
► Kiwi slices are great for wings and fins.
► Make arms and legs out of liquorice strips.
► Use raisins or chocolate beans for eyes.
► Almond flakes are just right for ears and wings.

Birthday cakes

You can leave out everything else, but no child's birthday party can be without a cake. Blowing out the candles, admiring the cake and cutting it up is the focal point of any birthday party. But it really doesn't have to be the focal point of your life for three weeks before.

Blowing out the candles is a much-loved tradition.

Ready-made cakes

If you are not a keen cook or can't cope with creating your own cake decorations, turn off the 'guilt' button and buy a cake. Most supermarkets stock a selection and you might be lucky and find one that matches your theme. Specialist cake shops will make one to your requirements, for a price, or there might be someone in your area who is happy to bake cakes for parties. If you are not confident about making or baking your own cake, this is a sensible choice because you won't want it to go wrong.

Shaped cakes

You can buy (or, better, hire) cake tins in shapes such as numbers, flowers, squares, rectangles, hearts or hexagons from cake shops. They are also available in a variety of different sizes. By using one of these specially shaped tins, you can make (or buy) a basic cake mix and bake it into your desired shape. Or you could use the cake mix to bake a tray cake and then cut out your desired shape using a template.

Tray-bake cake

Preheat the oven to 180°C/350°F/Gas mark 4 and grease and line a roasting tin measuring about 33 x 25cm (13 x 10in). Beat together 350g (12oz) softened butter or margarine, 450g (1lb) self-raising flour, 3 tsp baking powder, 350g (12oz) caster sugar and 3 tbsp milk until you have a smooth mixture. Pour it into the tin, smoothing the top. Bake for about 35 minutes until cooked – test by pressing the centre with your fingertips. If it springs back, it is cooked. Leave it in the tin to cool.

Make a paper template of the shape you want, keeping it as simple as possible. Rest the template on the cake and cut around it with a sharp knife. Alternatively, cut the cake into blocks, which could be used to build any manner of shapes. These can be 'glued' with icing sugar, jam or melted chocolate.

Make a template of your chosen cake shape, lay it on top of the cooled cake and cut gently around the edge with a sharp knife.

No-bake shaped cakes

Another way to create a shaped cake is to buy slabs and other shapes of cake to cut up and make into your own design. You could use:

▶ Madeira cake for building blocks such as the base.
▶ Swiss rolls for cylinder shapes like a traditional train shape.
▶ Mini Swiss rolls for wheels.
▶ Chocolate-covered marshmallows for small domes.

must know

Decorating materials
Straight lines: chocolate matchsticks
Circles: round biscuits, marshmallows
Small items for making patterns: chocolate drops, beans and buttons, hundreds and thousands, sugar or chocolate strands, sugar flowers, silver balls, candied fruit sticks, jelly diamonds, angelica
For writing: use writing icing (it needs a steady hand) or alphabet letters

Once the shape is cut and the icing is on, anything goes sa far as cake decoration is concerned! Here are a variety of ideas to act as a starting point. Be as specific or abstract as you like.

'Glue' them together with icing sugar, jam or melted chocolate and once you've made your shape, cover it in icing (see right) or melted chocolate, then complete the decoration.

Decorating cakes

One very simple and effective option is to purchase a simple birthday cake and add your own personalized decorations. These could include:

▶ Writing the child's name in icing.

▶ Adding edible decorations such as sweets.

▶ Adding decorations to match the theme, such as a toy train or jewellery (just make sure you remove it before you serve the cake).

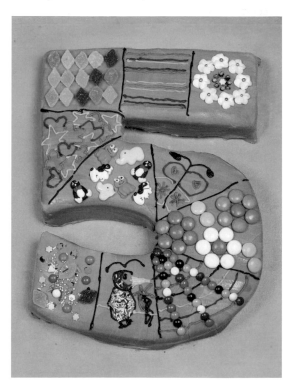

If you've made your own cake you will, of course, also want to decorate it. Start with the icing and then move on to the fun part with the myriad different decorating bits and pieces that are available in supermarkets. Lots of specialist books are available with ideas for decorating cakes, many of which feature moulding icing.

Icing

Icing creates a smooth, consistent finish, which can then be decorated if you wish.

Butter icing: This has a softer texture, so decorations can be set into it, but it has a richer taste than glacé icing, which will be soft enough to hold decorations until it dries. To make, see page 158.

Glacé icing: Sift 225g (8oz) icing sugar into a bowl, then slowly mix in 2 tbsp warm water until you have icing of the consistency you want. Add food dye to colour it. For chocolate icing, use 175g (6oz) icing sugar and 50g (2oz) drinking chocolate powder.

Ready-to-roll regal: Available in white and small packets of coloured, this gives a smooth finish to your cake. It is easy to colour with food dye or by mixing together different pre-coloured icings. If you find you become enamoured with making icing models, coloured sugar paste in a huge variety of colours is available from more specialist outlets.

Candles

There is an amazing array of candles to choose from: different colours and patterns, shapes such as numbers, sparkly burners, joke candles that re-light themselves, and even candles that play tunes.

watch out!

Candle safety
It is worth taking a few simple precautions with birthday candles to keep everyone safe:
▶ Use candle holders to put the candles in place on the cake. You don't want wax to dribble onto the cake.
▶ If any children have long hair, tie or hold it back: hair catches fire easily.
▶ Watch out for hanging fabric from clothing as it could catch fire.
▶ Streamers and other paper debris are another fire hazard that should be removed from the table before lighting the candles.

Smoothies and shakes

It's well known that fizzy, sugary, additive-laden drinks can get children very wound up and over-active. Since they will be excited enough just by being at a party, it is worth serving drinks that they will enjoy, but that don't run the risk of pushing them over the edge into a wild frenzy.

<table>
<tr><td>

good to know

Smoothies
Try these combinations/additions:
▶ Frozen strawberries with pineapple juice.
▶ Frozen chopped banana with pineapple juice.
▶ Adding a chopped banana to the blender mix to give the drink a smoother texture.
▶ Adding creamed coconut to improve the texture.

</td></tr>
</table>

Smoothies

You can make a variety of smoothies by blending a cup of fruit yogurt with the same quantity of fruit and 150ml (¼ pint) fruit juice. If you make a few different ones, the children could play a blindfold tasting game to see if they can identify the flavours. Follow these tips:

▶ Blend the fruit first then add the liquid ingredients.
▶ Fresh, tinned (drain first) or frozen fruits are quick and easy to use in a smoothie.
▶ Once the mixture is evenly blended, add ice cubes, two at a time, until the blender sounds smooth, or you can use ice-cold water or fruit juice.
▶ If the shake or smoothie is too thin, add fruit or ice. If it's too thick, add more liquid.

Shake your own smoothie

This could be a fun part of the party, as everyone can make their own drink provided you've got enough empty screw-top jars. Into each jar put 6 sliced strawberries and 1 tsp caster sugar. Mash them a bit with a spoon, add 200ml (7fl oz) milk, screw on the top (an adult should check the lid is tight at this point!) and shake it like crazy. Drink through a straw.

Pink smoothie

This is really fruity. For two drinks you'll need 4 strawberries, a sliced peach or nectarine, and a chopped-up small banana. Put these in a blender with a 150g (5oz) pot of fruit yogurt, 1 tsp honey and 150ml (¼ pint) fruit juice. You can, of course, substitute different fruits (mango is good).

Fruit shake

To make two banana shakes, put a chopped banana in the blender with 4 scoops chocolate or vanilla ice cream, then add 300ml (½ pint) milk and whiz it all up. Serve with an extra scoop of ice cream. For strawberry shake, use strawberry ice cream with 6 chopped strawberries.

Fruit smoothies make a really appealing and healthy drink.

Thick chocolate shake

Blend 6 scoops vanilla ice cream with 225ml (8fl oz) milk, 50g (2oz) milk chocolate chips and 4 cream-filled chocolate sandwich biscuits.

Party drinks

Cola, squash and (dare we say) water are fine, of course, but the these drink ideas will have more impact. As they are a bit different, suggest the children try a sip before filling their glasses.

Swizzle sticks transform a drink into a party cocktail.

Creamy cola

For a creamy cola, mix 600ml (1 pint) cola drink with 4 scoops vanilla ice cream and 1 tbsp lemon juice.

Foaming apple

Blend 4 scoops vanilla ice cream with 450ml (16fl oz) apple juice (or orange juice for variety) for a healthy foaming drink. Spice it up with a dash of cinnamon.

Spicy apple

Mix 600ml (1 pint) chilled milk with 4 scoops vanilla ice cream and 50g (2oz) apple purée. Add cinnamon and vanilla essence to taste.

Licuado

A licuado is a blended drink from Mexico made from fruit and milk. The basic recipe is 300ml (1/2 pint) each of chilled milk and juice plus plenty of ice and any available chopped fruit.

Mead

Here is a non-alcoholic version of an age-old drink, which would be perfect for a party with knights and princesses (page 50). Mix blackcurrant juice with hot water in the usual proportions. Pour onto sultanas and serve as a warm drink.

Home-made slush

You'll need to get the timing right if you want to serve this during the party, but it is great for a hot day. Try it out a few days before the party. In a freezable container, mix 600ml (1 pint) orange juice with 1 tsp lemon juice and 2 tbsp caster sugar. Put on the lid and pop it in the freezer for an hour. Then take it out and stir it to break up the ice crystals before returning the tub to the freezer for 2 hours. Now it is ready to enjoy.

Punch box

▶ You can make fizzy punch by mixing cranberry juice, frozen or fresh orange juice with bits in, and ginger ale.

▶ Add green and blue food colouring to change the colour – great for a Halloween party.

▶ A half-and-half mix of tomato juice and orange juice makes a satisfyingly 'bloody' drink.

▶ Make a layered punch by first pouring in grenadine (a thick juice made from pomegranates), and then gently adding lemonade or juice on top.

---

must know

Serving drinks

▶ Serve drinks only when the children are already sitting down at the table.

▶ Plastic glasses are so much safer (and cheaper!) than those made of glass.

▶ Use small glasses and don't fill any glasses to the top – it just risks spillages.

▶ There's no harm in watering down any drink to reduce its sugar and additive content.

▶ Kids love using straws, especially novelty bendy or twisty ones.

▶ Place an adult in charge of serving drinks from a drinks station. Some children can get very carried away when they have the chance to keep pouring drinks for themselves.

7 Running the party

Professional party organizers train for years under the watchful eye of experts. You're probably doing it with little or no experience and under the watchful eyes of (perhaps critical) parents. This chapter offers advice on organizing yourself, the children and any helpers you bring in (and you should!). It is hard work, but if you've come this far quite happily, the party ought to be the bit you enjoy the most, because everyone, including you, will have a great time.

Take charge

Holding a party is a big task. Don't be afraid to have lists so you can make sure everything happens when it should, and don't be afraid to ask for help because you can't do everything yourself!

Managing groups of children

You may be incredibly well organized and have everything set up for the party, but the biggest challenge can be taking charge of a group of children. They are rightly excited and expecting to have fun, but you will want to ensure they are all safe and that no one has grounds to feel upset.

When you are dealing with a group of children, using their names is important, so if you don't know them, you could ask everyone to wear a name badge. You can tie the badges in with your party theme, and don't forget to have one each for you and for your helpers. These tips will also help:

▶ Use a gentle voice. If you are quiet, the children are more likely to be calm.

▶ Introduce yourself and any other helpers.

▶ If there are parts of the house that are out of bounds for the party (for example, the upstairs bedrooms), make this clear. You could reinforce it with polite signs.

▶ Politely explain any other rules the children need to follow. They are used to having rules set when they are somewhere new.

▶ Tell them where the toilets are. Show younger children where to go.

▶ Keep smiling! Unfamiliar faces are friendlier that way.

When you want children to come through to another room or

Large groups of children are more manageable sitting on the floor.

outdoors, it is worth finding a way to
send them in small groups to avoid
a crush. Some ways to do this are:

▶ Inviting them out by name.

▶ Saying, 'Put your hand up if
you've got a green front door' or
other variations like, 'If you like
fish' or, 'If you walked here.' Send
that group out first, then choose
the next.

▶ Invite a child to say the names of
who should go next.

If possible, have someone in the next room ready to
welcome them.

**Switch between
lively and calm
games so children
don't get over
excited.**

Handling problems

Sometimes children have difficulty behaving nicely, especially
when they are excited and in unfamiliar surroundings.

▶ First, remember that not every child is used to following
your ways – expectations may be very different in their own
home life.

▶ If the child is not behaving as you would like, but with no risk
of hurting another child or his feelings, and is safe themselves,
it is best to ignore the behaviour.

▶ However, if you really feel she is spoiling other children's
enjoyment and you need to speak with her, quietly ask her to
come to you, or bend down near her, so that you can speak to
her in a whisper.

▶ However tempted you are, try not to shout – it raises the
stakes and can upset children. Quietly explain that you want
everyone to have a good time and tell the child in question how
she can help this to happen. There's no point getting into a
major confrontation: but you might make a mental note not to
invite her again!

Help!

It makes so much sense to have at least one, preferably two or three, helpers at your party, for reasons of safety, convenience, efficiency and perhaps – most importantly – your sanity.

Why you need helpers

Looking after groups of children can be stressful. The first priority is safety, and having a helper gives you someone to turn to if a child is injured or in danger. If the party is being held outdoors, like a park, or in an indoor public place such as a soft-ball park, you want the reassurance of knowing where the children are at all times, and who they are with.

Older children can be really helpful in keeping young ones involved in the game.

Who can you ask?

You need people who either know you, or some of the children, fairly well. Obvious candidates include other adults in your family, and friends and parents of some of the children at the party. If the birthday child has brothers or sisters, they can be helpful if they are older than the children attending the party. Siblings are especially useful in helping shy children or anyone who needs reassurance during a game – some children are happier being comforted or helped by an older child than

by an adult, who they may find big and threatening. If you have a childminder or regular babysitter who knows your child and maybe some of the others, she (or he) could be a good choice, and if you are paying her, you won't feel guilty about giving her a set of jobs to do.

Whoever you use, agree in advance what their main role will be. Of course they should be on hand to deal with any difficulties, like an injured or upset child, but if they have a specific job to do, they will feel more useful, and you will be reassured that one job is taken care of. You should discuss and agree the roles of each helper in advance. These could include:

▶ Taking care of coats and shoes.

▶ Painting faces of guests.

▶ Taking photographs (make sure the helper knows how to use your camera).

▶ Attaching name labels.

▶ Preparing food such as sandwiches or hot dishes.

▶ Laying the food table.

▶ Running some of the games.

▶ Manning the music station during musical games.

▶ Taking care of a guest who you feel may be particularly shy.

It would also help if you followed these guidelines:

▶ If possible, have the helpers arrive before the party starts so that you don't have any last-minute panics.

▶ If the guests are to wear name labels, make some for you and your helpers, and be sure to introduce the helpers to children soon after they arrive.

▶ If you are going to a venue away from home, make sure you and the helpers all have each other's mobile phone number.

▶ Provide food and drink for your helpers (it needn't be the same as the children's food) – they may appreciate being given an alternative to the party fare they are dishing out!

▶ Be sure to thank them, possibly with a small gift. You may want their cooperation again next time!

Countdown

Successful parties rarely just happen, they need to be planned. This should not be too much of a chore because working out what to do and getting it done are part of the fun and add to the sense of anticipation.

The birthday child

Birthdays are important to children, and part of the fun of a party is the anticipation and preparation for it. Try to keep your child as involved as possible in getting ready for the party. She can help decide the theme, venue and entertainer, help make or choose invitations, think about the type of food to serve, and so on.

The more your child is involved, the more she feels it is her party.

Plan ahead

Eight weeks ahead
Choose the theme
Set the date and time
Book the venue and the entertainer

Four weeks ahead
Decide who to invite
Make or buy invitations

Three weeks ahead
Send out invites
Book the helpers

One week ahead
Chase up people who haven't replied
Check special food requirements
Confirm booking with venue and entertainer
Finalize your list of games and check you've got the right equipment
Book food deliveries
Check you've got anough seats for everyone to sit down

22 MOV 0580
23 DSC 0582 / MOV 0584
24 MOV 0593
25 MOV 0599
26
27 MOV 0603
28 MOV 0605
29
30 MOV 0616
1 MOV 0623
2 MOV 0660
3
4 MOV 0706
5
6
7
8 DONE

9
10
11
12 MOV 0738
13

ridge or freezer

:side

ısport

Get the table ready and shut the door until it is time to eat!

However, what you want is involvement, not obsession, so encourage him to balance these jobs with other activities, and if all you seem to talk about is the birthday party, you could agree that you will chat about it once a day, maybe after your evening meal. Remind your child than plans sometimes need to be changed and you might need to alter what happens, even during the party itself – some children find this difficult to understand and do not like change.

On the day

There are lots of jobs to do before the party starts, so try to share them out. The birthday child can reasonably be expected to do as much as he can to make his party a success, and other family members should be able to chip in, too.

Jobs for the morning

Take pets to a safe place away from the noise and bustle
Prepare the rooms to be used for the party
Decorate the room
Collect helium-filled balloons
Inflate air-filled balloons
Set up the party table
Prepare the fresh food
Prepare food for the adult helpers
Clear a space for where gifts will be put
Collect cake
Decorate the cake

Order of events

Welcome the guests
Collect presents
Play a calm ice-breaker game
Play a quiet game
Open presents
Play a lively game or two
Food
Lively game
Quiet game
Entertainer
Blow out candles on cake
Lively game
Quiet game
Hand out party bags or do
    lucky dip
Wave goodbye/deliver guests
    home
Relax!

Test the party blowers!

Typical party schedule

The lists on pages 179–81 may look as if your party should be run with military precision, but they are really just checks to make sure you don't forget something important amid all the hubbub of a party. It is also quite hard to think straight when you are setting up a game, wondering if the sausage rolls are burning, and keeping a caring eye on a shy guest. If you hire an entertainer, he is likely to arrive just before the party begins – factor this into your plans.

This lists are designed to keep you organized so that you can relax and have fun too. But once you have a clear idea of everything that should happen, you decide as the party progresses whether anything needs changing. For example:

▶ If the children don't seem to be enjoying the games, or only a few are participating, change them or do something else.

▶ If everyone around the food table seems restless, take a break from eating, play a game outside and then come in for the second course. Any teacher will tell you, just because an activity is well planned, it is not an automatic success: you are dealing with individuals and that demands flexibility.

Present and correct

Some people prefer their child not to open presents during the party as it can be distracting and take up a lot of time. However, guests like to see their presents being opened and having the chance to be thanked at the time. They enjoy seeing other children's reactions to their gifts.

There are also some parents who argue that children have plenty of toys and games these days and that expecting more gifts at a party is a sign of over-consumption. They suggest instead that the birthday invitation should request donations for a specified charity, such as sponsoring an essential farm animal for a village in a poorer part of the world. The decision is obviously up to you and your child; just make sure that you communicate anything out of the norm to the parents of the children coming.

Remember to allow time in your plans for an entertainer to set up his stall.

After the party

Phew! However prepared they were for the party, most parents feel a sense of relief when it is over. Everybody had a good time, your child enjoyed a memorable party, and now you can have a rest. There are just a few 'i's to dot and 't's to cross.

Feed yourself and your family

It can be very easy to focus on the party food and forget about other people's requirements, including your own. You may plan to tuck into whatever is left from the party fare, but this may not be to everybody's taste and the visiting hordes may have been particularly ravenous. Treat yourself! Either have something prepared before that you can just heat up, buy in a take away or, even better (and if you're not too exhausted), go out for a family meal. In an ideal world, you would return to a beautifully cleaned and tidied house, but that might not happen.

The 'thank yous'

With luck, you remembered to make a list of who gave what as a present, which now means you get the chance to utter the dreaded question, 'Have you written your "thank you" notes yet?' It is a chore, but people of all ages appreciate being thanked properly for a present that they may have thought long and hard about when choosing. It doesn't have to be a long, formal letter. Young children might like to do a drawing of the present and send that with a short line of thanks. Older children might be able to 'cheat' and produce a standard 'thank you' letter on the computer, which they then personalize for each recipient. If you have the time and inclination, you and/or your child could make some 'thank you' cards.

Try to get this job done within a week – recipients appreciate promptness, and it will seem more of a chore if you try to recall who gave what three weeks down the line. If you took pictures during the party, this is a chance to print an extra copy of a suitable photograph and send it with the 'thank you' note.

Finally, try to get some casual feedback from your child about the party – it will help if you run another one in the future, or help you to decide, 'Next year we take two friends to the zoo!'

Keep a note of who gave what as it helps when it's time to write those 'thank you' letters.

There are thousands of websites offering children's party supplies, many with directories of party organizers, entertainers and venues and food recipes.

Sites ending with the letters '.com' are mostly American, but they can be useful because some of the advice they offer is helpful, especially for games ideas, and some have links to UK suppliers.

Where phone numbers are available, they are supplied.

Party organizers
www.kids-party.com/partyplannersorganisers.shtml
scotlandinter.net/childrensparties.htm
www.partypages.co.uk (includes a directory of party organizers)

Party entertainers
homepage.ntlworld.com/services/Party-Supplies/party-entertainers.htm
www.entsweb.co.uk/entertainers/childrens/
www.childrenspartyshows.co.uk
tel: 01753 518266

General party supplies and advice
UK sites
www.allparty.co.uk tel: 0870 889 0303
www.bbc.co.uk/cbeebies
www.bhg.com
www.celebrations-party.co.uk
tel: 0844 555 2028
www.eventwise.co.uk tel: 020 7386 5000
www.familiesonline.co.uk
(advice, products and recipes)
www.forparentsbyparents.com/info_parties_goods.html
www.funinabox.co.uk tel: 01277 233778

hwww.funpartysupplies.co.uk
tel: 01277 233778
www.greatlittleparties.co.uk tel: 01908 266080
www.nonstopparty.co.uk
www.party2u.co.uk tel: 01530 834734
(who kindly supplied many of the props and decorations for this book)
www.partybox.co.uk tel: 01483 486000
www.partydelights.co.uk tel: 0161 776 1133
www.partydirectory4kids.co.uk
tel: 01252 851601
www.partydomain.co.uk tel: 0870 889 0303
www.partypacks.co.uk tel: 01749-890634
www.partypieces.co.uk
tel: 01635 201844
www.partytreasures.co.uk tel: 01324 495292
www.partyzone.co.uk tel: 01277 226999
www.turretsandtiaras.co.uk tel: 01484 665100
www.ukpartyshop.co.uk tel: 0845 166 2683

Non-UK sites
www.buzzle.com (has some good advice on face painting at parties)
www.birthdaydirect.com
kidspartysurvivalguide.com (has a UK link)
www.parenthub.com/parenting/birthdays.htm
www.birthdayexpress.com

Party bags and novelties
www.novelties-direct.co.uk
tel: 08453 31 34 31
www.rainbowpartybags.co.uk
tel: 020 8644 0611
www.theglowcompany.co.uk
tel: 01302 771 446

Balloon suppliers
www.ballisticblue.com
balloonland.co.uk tel: 0800 781 3448
www.signatureballoons.com
tel: 01635 201844

Craft ideas and equipment (including card supplies)

www.potterypainting.co.uk tel: 02380 904464
www.kidzcraft.co.uk tel: 01793 327022
www.thescrapbookhouse.com tel: 01608 643332
www.crafts-beautiful.com
www.readicut.co.uk tel: 01924 810810
www.ss-services.co.uk tel: 01789 765323

Costumes

www.charliecrow.co.uk tel: 01782 417133
www.sureshots.co.uk
www.wackywardrobe.com tel: 01295 278759
(who kindly lent us costumes for this book)
www.directory.justfancydress.co.uk
tel: 0117 9693815

Games ideas

www.eventwise.com
www.funandgames.org
www.gameslinks.com
www.holidaycook.com/party-games
www.kids-partycabin.com
www.partygamecentral.com
www.thefunplace.com
www.urbanext.uiuc.edu/party/games.
www.child-tea-party-game-ideas.com/
tea-party-games.html
www.holidaycook.com/party-games/
www.gameslinks.com/Party_Games/
www.comeparty.co.nz

Cake recipes

cake.allrecipes.com
www.cadbury.co.uk tel: 0121 451 4444
www.eezplanit.com

Cake suppliers who deliver party cakes

amato.co.uk tel: 020 7734 5733
www.caketoppers.co.uk tel: 01252 350641
www.jane-asher.co.uk tel: 020 7584 6177
www.mariascakes.co.uk tel: 01424 435245

Useful books

Food
Annabel Karmel's Complete Party Planner (Ebury Press)
Children's Parties Juliet Moxley (Ebury Press)
50 Easy Party Cakes, Debbie Brown (Murdoch Books)
Parties for Kids, Judy Bastyra (Kingfisher Books)

Games
Great Big Book of Children's Games, Debra Wise (McGraw-Hill)
Kid's Party Games and Activities, Penny Warner (Meadowbrook Press)
Practical Parenting Party Games, Jane Kemp and Clare Walters (Hamlyn)

Face painting
Face Painting (Mini Maestro S.) (Top That Publishing Plc)
Five Minute Faces (Kingfisher Books)
Starting Face Painting (Usborne Publishing Ltd)
The Usborne Book of Face Painting, Chris Caudron (Usborne Publishing Ltd)
Wild Faces: Animal Face Painting (Kingfisher Books)

Index

Acknowledgments

Lyra Publications wish to thank the following for their help:
- All the models – Amy, Anna, Ashley, Billy, Claire, Floella, Georgia, Holly, Isobel, Josh, Juliet, Katie, Maxim, Naomi, Oliver, Sarah, Thea, Victoria and William – for their patience and enthusiasm.
- Sarah Childs-Carlile for the use of her garden.
- Paul Kybert, magician.
- Party2u (www.party2u.co.uk) for supplying party materials.
- The Scrapbook House (www.thescrapbookhouse.com) for supplying card materials.
- Wacky Wardrobe (www.wackywardrobe.com) for loaning costumes.
- The Thomas the Tank Engine cake on page 61 is photographed by permission of the Greencore Group.

⚙ **Collins** need to know?

Look out for these recent titles in Collins' practical and accessible need to know? series.

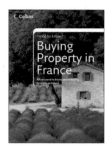

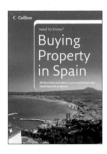

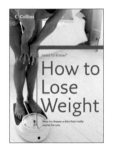

Other titles in the series:

Birdwatching
Body Language
Card Games
DIY
Dog Training
Drawing & Sketching
Golf
Guitar

Kama Sutra
Knots
Pilates
Speak French
Speak Italian
Speak Spanish
Stargazing
Watercolour

Weddings
Wood-Working
The World
Yoga
Zodiac Types

To order any of these titles, please telephone 0870 787 1732. For further information about all Collins books, visit our website: www.collins.co.uk